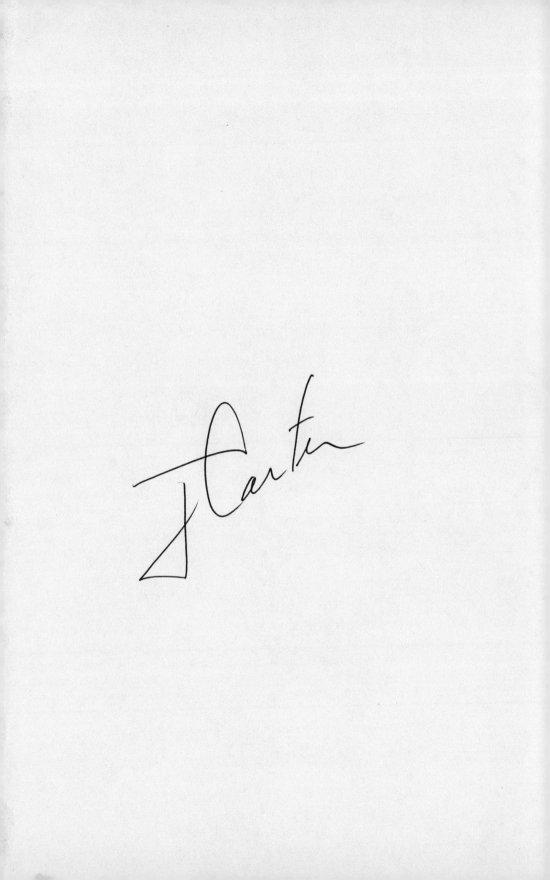

ALSO BY **Jimmy Carter**

An Outdoor Journal

Everything to Gain: Making the Most of the Rest of Your Life
(with Rosalynn Carter)

The Blood of Abraham: Insights into the Middle East

Keeping Faith: Memoirs of a President

A Government as Good as Its People

Why Not the Best?

Turning Point

TURNING POINT

A Candidate, a State,
and a Nation Come of Age

✶✶✶✶✶✶✶✶✶✶✶✶✶✶✶✶✶✶✶✶✶✶✶✶✶✶✶✶✶✶

JIMMY CARTER

TIMES 𝕿 BOOKS

All rights reserved under International and Pan-American Copyright
Conventions. Published in the United States by Times Books, a
division of Random House, Inc., New York, and simultaneously in
Canada by Random House of Canada Limited, Toronto.

Grateful acknowledgment is made to the *Atlanta Journal* and the
Atlanta Constitution for permission to reprint an editorial entitled
"Cloud Over Georgetown" from the October 30, 1962, issue of the
Atlanta Journal, page 22. Reprinted by permission from the *Atlanta
Journal* and the *Atlanta Constitution*.

Library of Congress Cataloging-in-Publication Data

Carter, Jimmy.
Turning point : a candidate, a state, and a nation come of age /
Jimmy Carter.—1st ed.
p.   cm.
Includes index.
ISBN- 0-8129-2079-1
1. Carter, Jimmy, 1924– . 2. Georgia—Politics and
government—1951– I. Title.
E873.A3   1992
973.926'092—dc20   92-53671

BOOK DESIGN BY CATHRYN S. AISON

Manufactured in the United States of America
9 8 7 6 5 4 3 2

For Maggie, Jeremy, and Jamie

CONTENTS

✫✫✫✫✫✫✫✫✫✫✫✫✫✫✫✫✫✫✫✫✫✫✫✫✫✫✫✫✫✫✫✫✫

ACKNOWLEDGMENTS

✯✯✯✯✯✯✯✯✯✯✯✯✯✯✯✯✯✯✯✯✯✯✯✯✯✯✯✯✯

I have relived many exciting events in writing this book, centered on the election year of 1962. Some of the memories are too vivid ever to forget, while others had become confused with the passage of thirty years. As would be expected, Rosalynn and I retained our scrapbooks and other personal records of those days, and these have provided the foundation for the account. Since most of the key players in the drama are still living, I have also been able to consult with them extensively. It has been especially interesting to go back to Quitman County, Georgia, where most of the action took place, and to reminisce with the people who still live there. Regardless of whether they were my supporters or opponents in those earlier days, all of them have been willing to spend a few hours recalling what was to all of us a series of historic experiences.

It was surprising how many of the attorneys had retained their records of the legal cases, and they were gracious enough to review their files and make the pertinent ones available to me.

Dr. Steve Hochman was of special help. He had assisted me in reviewing White House records when I wrote my memoir, *Keeping Faith*, in 1981 and has been my special assistant during the past decade while I lectured regularly at Emory University. When I decided to write *Turning Point*, Steve continued to help me. He also recruited an outstanding Emory student, Scott Bertschi, who studied the legal history of the "one man, one vote" Supreme Court ruling, perused the files of newspapers published during the summer and fall of 1962, and presented all this information to me so I could use it most effectively. Research was conducted at the Georgia Department of Archives and History, the Jimmy Carter Library, the Emory University Library, and the University of Georgia Library.

My assistant, Faye Dill, played an integral role in the preparation of this book. She located many of the people involved, arranged my interviews with them, obtained approval for the use of personal and copyrighted texts and photographs, and helped resolve differences between me and the editors.

Peter Osnos and Paul Golob, Times Books editors, helped me arrange this material in a more logical and orderly fashion, and prodded me to expand on some of the incidents so that they would be described in a more understandable way.

I am grateful to all of them, and I hope this text will do justice to their good work.

CAST OF CHARACTERS

✶✶✶✶✶✶✶✶✶✶✶✶✶✶✶✶✶✶✶✶✶✶✶✶✶✶

(in order of appearance)

ERNEST VANDIVER, governor of Georgia, 1959–1963.

BEN FORTSON, Georgia secretary of state, brother of Warren Fortson.

GRIFFIN BELL, judge of the U.S. Court of Appeals for the Fifth Circuit, member of the two judicial panels that heard the county unit and reapportionment cases, Rosalynn's cousin, former law partner of Charles Kirbo.

CARL SANDERS, president pro tem of the state Senate and successful Democratic candidate for governor in 1962.

JOE HURST, state representative from Quitman County, chairman of the county Democratic committee, employee of the state Department of Agriculture, supporter of Homer Moore.

HOMER MOORE, my opponent in the race for the state Senate seat representing the Fourteenth Senatorial District, warehouseman and hardware store owner in Richland, Georgia.

ROBERT McKENZIE, incumbent state senator from Quitman County, also representing Stewart and Webster counties.

RALPH BALKCOM, farmer, Quitman County school superintendent, Rosalynn's cousin, who observed the voting in Quitman County on my behalf.

SAM SINGER, state representative from Stewart County, campaign manager for Homer Moore and his representative on the recount committee, warehouseman and former mayor of Lumpkin, Georgia.

JOHN POPE, manufacturer of burial vaults from Americus, who observed the voting in Quitman County on my behalf.

ROBERT ELLIS, Quitman County ordinary (probate judge).

DOC HAMMOND, close associate of Joe Hurst, assistant poll manager for state senatorial election in Quitman County.

LUKE TEASLEY, reporter for the *Columbus Enquirer*.

TOMMY GARY, U.S. peanut warehouse inspector, son of the late Senator Loren Gary of Quitman County.

LOREN WHITAKER, chief poll manager and longtime supporter of Joe Hurst, whose daughter worked the polls for the state senatorial election in Quitman County.

WARREN FORTSON, my attorney in the election dispute, brother of Ben Fortson.

J. B. FUQUA, chairman of the state Democratic party, owner of television and radio stations in Augusta, close associate of Carl Sanders.

WINGATE DYKES, Sumter County Democratic chairman, my father's lawyer, brother-in-law and supporter of Tom Marshall.

TOM MARSHALL, brother-in-law of Wingate Dykes and state superior court judge for the Southwest Judicial Circuit, who made a midnight ruling in our case.

JOHN PENNINGTON, investigative reporter for the *Atlanta Journal*.

JESSE BOWLES, lawyer for Homer Moore and Joe Hurst.

BILLY HORNE, a friend of mine from Americus, my representative on the recount committee.

CARL CROW, state superior court judge for the Albany Judicial Circuit, chairman of the recount committee.

CHARLES KIRBO, my lawyer, former law partner of Griffin Bell.

DAVID GAMBRELL, junior partner in Charles Kirbo's law firm.

PETER ZACK GEER, executive secretary to the governor, successful Democratic candidate for lieutenant governor in 1962.

GEORGE BUSBEE, state representative from Dougherty County, Homer Moore's lawyer, close associate of Governor Carl Sanders.

GEORGE D. STEWART, executive secretary of the state Democratic party.

ROBERT HAWKINS, Sumter County ordinary (probate judge).

INTRODUCTION

✷✷✷✷✷✷✷✷✷✷✷✷✷✷✷✷✷✷✷✷✷✷✷✷✷✷✷✷✷✷✷

This book is about my first campaign for public office. I was a naive thirty-eight-year-old farmer and small-town businessman who wanted to be part of the new openness and reform in the life of my state and nation that was being promised in 1962. Instead, I confronted forces of electoral fraud and corruption that are almost unimaginable today. I received a startling education in politics, one that set the tone for my future career.

At that time, America was on the precipice of change, facing a future that no one could predict and that would bring into direct conflict the greatest fears of some and the most profound hopes and dreams of others. The racially segregated world that had existed since the War Between the States was about to undergo a transformation nearly as great as had been brought about by the war itself.

In May 1954, the U.S. Supreme Court had ruled in *Brown v. Board of Education* that the common practice of "separate but equal" schooling for black and white children was inherently discriminatory and unconstitutional. However, with the political system heavily dominated by rural white voters, politicians and school officials in the South were free to condemn and then largely ignore this decision. Early in 1955, for instance, the Georgia General Assembly passed a "states' rights" law that forbade the use of state funds by any school system that dared to integrate its classrooms.

Nevertheless, the civil rights movement began to gain momentum, and racial tensions increased. The same year, a young black man, Emmett Till, was killed in Mississippi for allegedly whistling at a white woman, and Martin Luther King, Jr., helped organize the Montgomery bus boycott after Rosa Parks was arrested for refusing to give up her seat to a white man. The Ku Klux Klan and White Citizens' Councils flourished throughout the South as racial battle lines were drawn.

In Albany, Georgia, only forty miles from my home in Plains, Dr. King began in 1960 a sustained but unsuccessful effort to integrate the white churches. On occasion, peaceful demonstrations by black and a few white integrationists were held in Americus, our county seat. When the demonstrators refused to obey police orders to disband their vigils, their leaders were arrested and confined in the local jails for a few days until they paid bail and were released. This process was repeated until it seemed to be a routine operation, well under control, that might go on almost indefinitely.

Despite the growing prominence of Dr. King's Southern Christian Leadership Conference, the most significant target of concern among segregationists during those years came from a different source. It seemed that real changes might be forthcoming when in 1960 black students began sit-in demonstrations, demanding service alongside whites at public lunch counters. These confrontations were more aggressive and aroused a tremendous response from young and more militant demonstrators.

The Student Nonviolent Coordinating Committee (SNCC) was formed in May of that year, with leaders who would later become famous, including Marion Barry, Julian Bond, Marian Wright, Lonnie King, Clarence Mitchell, John Lewis, and James Forman, the executive secretary. Their slogan was "Jail—No Bail!" Leaders of older organizations, such as the Congress of Racial Equality, the National Association for the Advancement of Colored People, and the Southern Christian Leadership Conference, supported SNCC's efforts and participated personally in some of the sit-ins. Within two years, 70,000 students and other young people had been marshaled to challenge existing segregation laws in the Southeast and to encourage voter registration of black citizens. Thirty-six hundred of them were arrested during this period, and several were killed.

The days of orderly vigils, brief incarceration of demonstrators, quick bail, and little activist support were over. Many Southern political leaders were in a quandary about how to meet these new challenges to their segregated societies, and they responded in different ways. In Georgia, a relatively moderate lieutenant governor, Ernest Vandiver, had been elected governor in 1958 by appealing to the sentiments of rural white voters hostile to desegregation. Campaigning on the promise "No, not one!" Vandiver repeatedly pledged that no black child would attend a public school or college with white students so long as he was governor. However, when a federal judge ordered that two black students be admitted to the University of Georgia in 1961, Vandiver honored the ruling. Other Southern leaders, like George Wallace in Alabama and Ross Barnett in Mississippi, openly defied the federal courts and called for massive public resistance to any racial integration.

In all the Southern states, politicians had long relied on ancient laws and legislative malapportionment to protect the system of legal segregation. The foundation for this effort in Georgia (and in other states) was the county unit system, which allotted votes by counties, with little difference between those with large and small populations. This system ensured rural white domination of the electoral process by grossly diluting the influence of urban dwellers and black citizens. The system guaranteed that potential reformers would constitute a minority when laws that involved racial integration were considered. Another great benefit of the county unit system for political incumbents was that their own exaggerated power could not be diluted by a rapidly growing urban population.

Then, in March 1962, the "one man, one vote" ruling of the U.S. Supreme Court in *Baker v. Carr* sent shock waves through the nation's political structure. The decision effectively required that all citizens' votes have equivalent weight in choosing candidates for public office. The major difficulty was that the beneficiaries of the existing system were the ones now charged with the responsibility of changing it, reducing drastically the relative voting strength of their own constituents. It was understandable that governors and legislators would do everything possible to circumvent or postpone the effect of the Court's mandate, but federal judges forced its implementation during the same election year. Thus began the series of events that led to my first political campaign.

When Georgia laws were changed to require a special election to implement the "one man, one vote" ruling, I announced as a candidate for the state Senate. It happened to be October 1, 1962, the day that James Meredith attempted to enroll as the first black student at the University of Mississippi. Despite the presence of hundreds of federal troops, an uncontrollable mob action was encouraged by Governor Ross Barnett, resulting in two deaths and many injuries. It was a historic event, publicized throughout the world. My own announcement was buried even in our local newspaper, the *Americus Times-Recorder*.

✴ ✴ ✴

This book looks at Southern politics in microcosm, with glimpses of a more panoramic scene that encompasses the past lives of our state and nation, often at their worst. It includes at least a partial explanation of how good and honest people first introduced, then inherited and preserved, customs and laws that let a minority of white citizens retain political supremacy. A central figure in the book is a shrewd and incredibly powerful political boss, often benevolent, who considered the rural community his own and could not accept any encroachment on his domain.

While this story is an intriguing tale of political shenanigans, it also reflects the transformation of Georgia and America, for the system that was threatened with extinction was not confined to the Deep South. More than half our nation's state legislatures, in all regions, were elected by giving exaggerated weight to the votes of mostly white people in rural communities and were affected by *Baker v. Carr*. In some cases, particularly in communities where racial discrimination was not an exacerbating factor, it took many years for the distortions to be removed. In fact, the last vestige of a county unit system did not perish in New York City until 1989, when the U.S. Supreme Court declared the Board of Estimate (on which each borough had one vote, regardless of population) unconstitutional.

In Georgia, both the political and the social landscape were irreversibly changed by the "one man, one vote" ruling. The South of 1964 and 1966 was to be a very different place from the same region in 1960. The 1962 campaign marked a turning point—the first real defeat for the old system on its own turf—that helped to end the legalized system of white supremacy, rural domination of government, and deprivation of civil rights among our neighbors.

Later, as governor and then president, I was continually reminded by national and world events of these earliest days of my political life and the similar challenges that still confront people everywhere who search for justice, truth, human rights, and governments in which they can have confidence. Increasingly, I saw the historical as well as the personal significance of what had happened in this election. That is why I have always wanted to tell this story.

So, over the last few years, I have gone back to review these events. In addition to my own notes and records, I have studied the news reports of the time, drawing on the newspaper collections at the libraries of Emory University in Atlanta and the University of Georgia in Athens. Most interesting have been the personal interviews with key players in the drama, many of whom are still living. Both political allies and opponents of mine have been willing to share their memories and their musty files, giving me new, surprising, and sometimes disturbing insights into what occurred. Memories are still vivid, because of the trauma of the time and because of resulting events on a much broader stage. Those involved have not forgotten their own roles in history.

These pages describe strange happenings thirty years ago in a remote town of 860 people. Although the setting was quite small, a remarkable number of future political leaders were involved, including two men who would become governors of our state, a president of the United States, his chief adviser, a U.S. senator, a U.S. attorney general, and two justices of the Georgia supreme court (one the chief justice). In addition, the political lives of many people were transformed through the resulting shifts in laws and customs. Not all the participants went on to greater things; some of the principal actors in this drama were later convicted of felonies, served time in the federal penitentiary, and lost their rights to vote or hold office in a community that they were accustomed to dominate.

The final results of this drama were shaped by people in one small county in southwest Georgia who never became famous but who made an impact on history because of their courage and fears, their conflicting values and ambitions. Their actions were part of the great upheaval in American life that was the 1960s, and we are still struggling with the issues they confronted.

Turning Point

chapter 1

✶✶✶✶✶✶✶✶✶✶✶✶✶✶✶✶✶✶✶✶✶✶✶✶✶✶✶✶✶✶✶✶✶

Citizens vs.

Counties

It is not easy to recall clearly my first interest in politics, but my family history almost guaranteed that I would someday find myself in the world of elections and law-making.

My mother's father, Jim Jack Gordy, was named after James Jackson, a Revolutionary War hero who accepted the British surrender of Savannah. Jackson was one of Georgia's first three U.S. congressmen and later served as governor and U.S. senator. Grandpa was active in local politics and was considered the most politically knowledgeable man in Webster and Stewart counties. Jim Jack would make his own predictions of election results, and on several occasions he let his educated guesses be put in the sheriff's safe early on election day, before the polls closed and the votes were tallied. Long before public opinion polls were developed, he had a reputation for knowing with remarkable accuracy what the people preferred. For a few years he lived on the farm next to ours in the Archery community, and he and my father kept the political scene thoroughly analyzed. Grandpa never ran for public office himself, but he was the postmaster during four presidential administrations and later was federal district revenue officer. Gaining these positions required nimble political footwork because at that time there was no civil service system. To the victors went the spoils, and to cast one's lot with the eventual winner was the only job insurance available.

As postmaster in the nearby town of Richland, my grandfather was the person who first conceived of rural free delivery of mail (RFD) and repeatedly made his proposals to Congressman Tom Watson to implement this idea through federal legislation. When this was finally accomplished in 1893, it was one of my grandfather's proudest achievements. When he was long past retirement age, Jim Jack held a doorkeeper's job at the state capitol just so he could continue to be involved in the political life of Georgia.

The first political rally I remember attending was for Congressman Charles Crisp, a native of nearby Americus, in the summer of 1932. As Speaker of the House of Representatives in Washington, he became an overconfident candidate for the U.S. Senate. Although my father and my grandfather were supporting his major opponent in this race, Governor Richard B. Russell, we went to the Speaker's kickoff rally because he was a resident of our home county—and because we wanted to see the fun. Crisp's plans went awry, however. He very carefully delayed the serving of a barbecue dinner until after his speech, wanting the crowd to give its undivided attention to the revelation of his platform. But a new bread-slicing machine had been installed on the fairgrounds for the occasion, and, since none of us had ever seen sliced bread before, most of the crowd gathered to watch the machine while only a few listened to the congressman orate.

This proved to be an omen. Although Speaker Crisp was the overwhelming favorite to win and had the backing of almost all the major newspapers in the state, Governor Russell successfully linked him to the Hoover administration and blamed him for many of the woes of the Great Depression. Russell also tied himself closely to the popular Franklin D. Roosevelt, whose nomination he had seconded at the Democratic national convention that year. Although he would later be famous as the chief defender of segregation, in this campaign Russell ran as a moderate, was endorsed by labor, made no reference to the race issue, and praised Roosevelt as a champion of human rights. He won handily.

My father, Earl Carter, often said that he too had been a strong supporter of Franklin Roosevelt in 1932, but Daddy fiercely opposed Roosevelt's subsequent imposition of controls on cotton acreage and his limitation on the number of hogs being prepared for market. When Daddy was forced to plow up knee-high cotton and to slaughter some of his growing pigs, he was deeply embittered and never again voted for the Democratic president. But in local and state elections, like all good Georgians, he continued to vote the straight Democratic ticket until his death.

Not having electricity on the farm, we would turn on

a large battery-operated radio to listen to special programs, but Daddy always insisted that we not waste the power. In 1936, the summer before I was twelve, our family huddled around the radio on the night of the Republican convention for several hours, until the battery went dead. What I remember most clearly is our carrying the big radio out into the yard, hooking it up to the automobile battery, letting the car engine run, and listening to the faraway delegates choose as their nominee Governor Alf Landon of Kansas, for whom my father later voted. I never did know whom my mother, Lillian, supported in the privacy of the voting booth during my boyhood years. It is as inconceivable to me that she voted Republican as that she deliberately contradicted my father in such an important matter.

Despite his aversion to much of Roosevelt's New Deal, Daddy welcomed rural electrification and quickly became active for the first time in the political world. He was one of the most influential members of the rural electric cooperative in our region. He and other farmers attended the national conventions and went to Washington on occasion to help defend the REA program, whose special low-interest loans permitted steady expansion of the service and provided an indirect rate subsidy to keep down the cost of electricity on farms. On the same trips he had no compunction about letting our members of Congress know of his opposition to many other New Deal programs.

✯ ✯ ✯

Back home in Georgia, my father was, above all, a Talmadge man. During these years, and for decades afterward, Georgians were divided roughly into two groups, depending on whether they were "Talmadge" or "anti-Talmadge." Eugene Talmadge, a brilliant politician from Telfair County in southeast Georgia, had been commissioner of agriculture and was elected governor in 1932 on the basis of his claim to represent the poor and rural folks of the state and his promise to preserve white supremacy. A spellbinding speaker and consummate political organizer and strategist, he aroused great crowds at his political rallies and inspired intense loyalty among his supporters.

Daddy would take his one-ton farm truck to Gene Talmadge's rallies and barbecues, its flat bed covered with straw and loaded down with our neighbors. When, for some reason, Daddy couldn't go himself, his truck would be there with its human payload. I went several times as a small boy, partly so the truck would be full and, I guess, because Daddy wanted me to learn about the political world. I'm not sure I learned the right things, but I enjoyed these excursions very much.

As many as 30,000 people, almost all men, would come to the rallies. Many of them would arrive early in the day to exchange political talk and to pass around their jugs of moonshine whiskey, as clear as water and more powerful than any whiskey that could have been bought in a store if Georgia had not been a totally dry state. We would wander around, looking at the dozens of hogs barbecuing on wire frames just above smoldering beds of oak and hickory coals, and visiting the booths where mementos of the day were being sold. Among the most popular items were bright red galluses, Gene Talmadge's trademark. One or two guitar or fiddle players or men's gospel quartets would be entertaining the swelling crowd, most of whom weren't in any hurry to see the event over and have to return home to the drudgery of Depression-era farm work.

Old photographs show that hats were the only standard item of clothing at the rallies, with men sporting gray fedoras or snap-brim Panama straws. There would be a good many overalls in the crowd, but most of the city folks and politicians would be wearing neckties and carrying their coats on their arms in the summer heat. There were always a few of the more agile supporters up in the trees near the speaker's platform, a claque whose job was to lead the frequent applause. They were really filling an unnecessary role, however, because the program and even the words of Talmadge's speech would be quite well known among his followers, with almost orchestrated responses at the appropriate times.

At a dramatic moment, the local politicians would end their preliminary speeches, and, with a musical fanfare, Gene Talmadge would be introduced. Not long after he began his usual humorous vituperations against the city of Atlanta and its newspapers, big banks, liberals, and voting blocs, the crowd would start shouting, "Take off your coat, Gene." The entreaty would grow in intensity until he finally shed his jacket and revealed his red suspenders. For some reason, this seemed to be the highlight of the entire event (with the exception of the barbecue dinner that followed), and the crowd would express its approval with wild applause. Talmadge was a populist, I guess, always promoting some choice proposals for cheap automobile tags, lower property taxes, retirement benefits for the elderly, or better school bus service or farm markets. One of his often repeated remarks was that he didn't care if he never had to campaign in a town with sidewalks or streetcars; his lot was cast with the voters in small towns and rural communities —where, he knew, there were enough county unit votes to keep him in office.

Talmadge's identification with the interests of small-town and rural voters was more than just a campaign slogan; it was the royal road to power in Georgia politics. In the nearly century and a half of Georgia's statehood, the number of counties had grown from 8 to 159, but the principles of voting based on counties, not voters, had withstood all challenges. Not only was the legislature apportioned by counties under the 1777 constitution but two men were also chosen from each county to elect the governor. Governors were elected by members of the legislature until 1825, when popular election was instituted. When the War Between the States was over, the federal government set two preconditions for the withdrawal of Northern troops and Georgia's readmission to the Union: first, the state would have to ratify the Thirteenth, Fourteenth, and Fifteenth amendments to the U.S. Constitution; second, Georgia would have to accept a new state constitution, passed under the leadership of a Republican governor.

It was this 1868 document that eliminated direct popular election for the governor and other state officers, establishing in its place the county unit system, a method of indirect election that was defended by claiming that it was somewhat akin to the electoral college in presidential elections. Except within individual counties, popular votes did not count. Instead, the constitution mandated that each of the six largest counties (changed in 1920 to eight), regardless of population, would cast six unit votes; more than a hundred of the smallest ones would have two votes apiece; and about thirty would have four. The state House of Representatives was also apportioned according to this 3-2-1 ratio.

By the time of the First World War, the value of a vote in Fulton County (Atlanta) had shrunk so much that it carried less than one-quarter the weight of an average vote in Georgia as a whole. The value of a vote in the smaller counties was, of course, much greater than the average. This disparity steadily increased as the Atlanta area continued to grow rapidly and some of the rural counties declined in population, with no adjustments being made in county unit votes. Thus, as Gene Talmadge well knew, voting strength and political power strongly favored rural communities and small towns at the expense of urban areas. Part of this trend resulted from the movement of people from farms to cities. The incumbent officials who would have had to modify the system were the very ones who enjoyed its benefits, and they had created laws and customs to keep control in their hands. The preservation of political power consequently became the driving force behind the county unit system. An unfortunate and not inadvertent aspect of the practice was that new voters, especially blacks, were not welcome to share democratic privileges equally with the more conservative white country folks.

Although the county unit system had evolved from early colonial times and had been established permanently by the Republican-dominated Reconstruction legislature, its main beneficiaries were the Democrats, who had won an overwhelming victory in the election of 1870 and have controlled Georgia politics ever since. For all practical purposes, the Democratic party soon supplanted the state government in the process for choosing state and local officials. Indeed, our state had almost completely melded the state government and the Democratic party into a single organism for conducting elections, an arrangement codified by the Neill Primary Act of 1917. Since the direct election of governors and other statewide candidates was forbidden by the state constitution, the act mandated that party delegates be selected in county primaries on the 3-2-1 ratio and cast their county's votes as a unit at the state Democratic convention. Only candidates chosen in this fashion would be certified by the secretary of state to go on the general election ballot as the party's nominees.

Whenever the governor and legislature faced legal challenges to the existing procedures or wished to change them without passing new laws, the simplest solution was for the state Democratic party to amend its rules. Since there was no viable Republican party, except for a small coterie of political opportunists who distributed national patronage when a member of their party was in the White House, a Democratic nomination for office was tantamount to election. In fact, the word *tantamount* was in the vocabularies of even illiterate adults and small children.

The Georgia Democratic party was endowed with extraordinary power, with the state government playing a supporting role. Only citizens on the state's list of qualified voters could participate in party primaries, which were run by Democrats and in which only Democrats could vote. However, state officials had to be at primary voting places on election day, clerks of the superior courts received the primary election results immediately after elections, and all penal laws covering general elections also applied to primaries. For all practical purposes, the state government and the Democratic party were inseparable and indistinguishable.

✭ ✭ ✭

Lined up against the Talmadge crowd were the more progressive candidates, whose fluctuating fortunes depended on the support of younger voters, those from the cities, the few liberals, at times some farmers, teachers, and elderly—all of whom could be outpromised by a moderate candidate—and the political chameleons who shifted their allegiance back and forth depending on which gubernatorial candidate seemed most likely to win the next election. Ralph McGill, editor and publisher of the *Atlanta Constitution* from 1942 until his death in 1969, was by far the best known and most influential liberal in the state, and he aroused almost uncontrollable rage among conservatives with his call for equal rights for black citizens. He also gave quiet encouragement to more progressive Georgians, who, at least in rural communities, rarely expressed their feelings to others.

In 1941, while serving his third two-year term as governor, Gene Talmadge left no doubt where he stood on the issue of race when he demanded the dismissal of the dean of the College of Education at the University of Georgia for supposedly advocating the racial integration of Georgia's schools. When the Board of Regents refused to follow the governor's orders, Talmadge purged the board and got rid of the dean and several other educators. In response, ernor, and he claimed the governorship, maintaining that the duly elected governor should be declared dead and that he was the successor. Ellis Arnall threw his support to Thompson and refused to give up the office until the legislature and courts could make a final decision. I was in the U.S. Navy then, serving on my first ship, and was deeply embarrassed by Georgia's three-governor controversy.

When the General Assembly members convened in January and finally counted all the write-in ballots, they were shocked to discover that irate supporters had given Carmichael 669 votes and that the almost completely unknown Republican candidate, D. Talmadge Bowers, had 637. Herman Talmadge had come in third and had missed the legislative runoff!

Then came a novel development. After almost three months, an additional 56 votes for Herman Talmadge, just enough to give him the highest number among the write-in contenders, were miraculously discovered in a box in his home county courthouse. Lyndon Johnson's supporters in Texas, who would help engineer his "landslide" victory by 87 votes for the U.S. Senate in 1948, may have learned a lesson from their Talmadge counterparts. In rapid succession, the Talmadge-dominated legislature chose Herman Talmadge as governor; Arnall refused to accept this decision; Talmadge forces changed all the locks and occupied the state capitol and the governor's mansion; Thompson set up his own governor's office in downtown Atlanta; and Herman Talmadge assumed the duties of Georgia's chief executive. Two months later, however, the Georgia supreme court ruled in favor of Thompson, who was permitted to serve but only for a two-year term. Herman

★ *15*

Talmadge never stopped campaigning, and in a special election in 1948 he, like his father, ran on a white supremacy platform. He had a narrow victory in popular votes but won overwhelmingly where it counted, in county units.

To the surprise of almost everyone, Herman Talmadge did a fine job as governor and was reelected to serve four more years. My daddy never wavered, so far as I know, in his support of the Talmadges. As governor, Herman Talmadge came down to Plains to make a high school graduation speech and spent the night with my parents. They became personal friends. Certainly by today's standards my father was a segregationist, as were nearly all the white citizens of the area, so far as I knew. It was a way of life that, in the early 1950s, had rarely been challenged in Georgia.

There was one notable exception: a totally integrated farming operation known as Koinonia (which means "brotherhood" in Greek) only nine miles southeast of Plains. A Baptist preacher, Dr. Clarence Jordan, had founded and maintained this community, in which black and white families lived, worked, and worshiped together as equals. Fiercely condemned by segregationists, the people at Koinonia suffered persistent economic boycotts and even physical attacks. They had to turn to distant markets to buy farm supplies and sell their produce to passing interstate motorists or by mail. Their roadside fruit and vegetable stand was burned by arsonists, and shots were fired into their homes and other buildings on several occasions. The highly publicized attacks bolstered their financial contributions from other parts of the country, and the farm seemed to thrive.

The only local person I knew who ignored the strict

social separation of the races was my mother. She was a registered nurse, and, in the rural community of Archery where I grew up during the Depression years, she met most of the medical needs of our neighbors. She knew they had no way to pay a doctor in town, and she didn't charge anything for helping them. When her black friends came to our home, she encouraged them to enter through the front door, and, as much as their discomfiture would permit, she treated them as equals. This was one of the few issues on which she defied my father—not blatantly, but in her quiet and persistent way. He had to learn not to acknowledge this breach of a rigid custom when it occurred.

As a naval officer during those years, and particularly in the close confines of a submarine, I naturally forgot or ignored racial distinctions, and this sometimes strained my relationship with Daddy when I came back to Plains on my infrequent leaves.

While I was serving on the USS *K-1*, a small submarine designed to go deep, stalk silently, and destroy other submarines, we went into port in Jamaica for some brief shore leave and recreation during an extended underwater cruise in the Caribbean. I happened to be the officer of the deck when the crew received an invitation from the British governor-general to a party in honor of our ship's visit. The aide who delivered the message told me that many of the young ladies in the community would be joining us for the evening. The officers and men were overjoyed at this news, and we began preparing for the event in high spirits. Quite a lot of money was paid to induce some of the more antisocial crew members to take the shipboard duties for the night of the party.

The same aide soon returned with a confidential message. The governor-general did not, of course, mean for our black crewmen to attend the ball. Jamaica was obviously as segregated as south Georgia in those days. When I informed our captain, William Andrews, he was dismayed. I suggested that we let the crew decide how to respond. They voted unanimously, and in the sailors' ribald but highly descriptive language, that we tell the Jamaican officials what they could do with their party. However, Captain Andrews observed protocol by merely withdrawing our acceptance of the invitation.

Back home on leave a month or so later and proud of what had happened, I told this story to my family. There was a moment of absolute silence, and then my father said, "The governor of Jamaica was absolutely right." He left the room without another word, and then my mother and I had a long talk. She finally got me to agree not to bring up race relations when Daddy was around.

Two years later, in 1953, I took leave from my duties and spent a couple of weeks at Daddy's bedside while he was dying of cancer, talking to him quietly about our family, his business and customers, and the general principles that had guided his life. A stream of visitors came to the front or back door, depending on whether they were white or black, to bring a gift of food or flowers, and I listened repeatedly as they recounted how their lives had been blessed by my father. Even my mother was surprised to learn of many of his secret acts of kindness and generosity.

My daddy had been active in the church, served on the county Board of Education, provided help to his warehouse customers far beyond his commercial obligations, and been a guiding light in almost every community project around Plains. Only a year earlier, the Talmadge supporters in our area had persuaded my father to run against the incumbent state representative, who was strongly anti-Talmadge and a thorn in the governor's side. Daddy won the election and almost immediately became a champion in the House of Representatives of vocational education. Although he served only a short time before his death, the local college library is named for him because of this good work.

✭ ✭ ✭

Rosalynn and I, with our growing family, had spent the first seven years of our marriage being transferred from one place to another as my career evolved in the U.S. Navy. I had increasingly attractive assignments, and we were happy with our life. For the last five years, I had been a submarine officer, my final duty having been under Admiral Hyman Rickover as senior officer of the crew that was building the second nuclear submarine, *Seawolf.* It was the best job a junior officer could have had.

Nevertheless, after my father died we decided to move back to Plains. More accurately, I made the decision over the almost violent opposition of my wife. I resigned my commission in October 1953 to come home, grow seed peanuts, buy and sell farm products to the farmers in the community, and assume some of the responsibilities that had made Daddy's life so admirable. It wasn't long before I had volunteered to take on most of these responsibilities, with the exception of running for political office.

Immediately after my father's funeral, a delegation of community leaders came to our house to tell my mother that she would have no opposition if she wished to take over Daddy's seat in the legislature. However, as a grieving widow, at that time still somewhat subdued by the influence of her dominant husband, she declined.

The group then offered to support Thad Jones, one of our Plains neighbors, a successful businessman, and a long-time friend of my parents. He finished out my father's term and ran successfully in subsequent elections, always without opposition. I did not think it appropriate for me to challenge him, and I would not have been successful if I had. Ours was a racially segregated society, and Thad was one of its most fervent champions. Later, this ardent segregationist was to help organize a boycott against our warehouse business because he considered Rosalynn and me to be in favor of racial integration.

Back in Plains from the navy, we received a quick education in agriculture and also in our neighbors' attitudes about social issues of the day. We worked hard to build up our business and to strengthen the ties of friendship that supplemented normal business relationships. Several times a year I would take a few carloads of our customers to the agricultural experiment station in Tifton, where we would spend all day learning better ways to grow peanuts, cotton, corn, and other crops; how to establish and maintain a good fish pond; how to grow pine trees more efficiently; how to improve our production of pork and beef; or how to build better fences. We sponsored similar courses for large numbers of local farmers at the schoolhouse in Plains, gave an annual prize to the outstanding Future Farmer of America, and tried to keep our equipment and stock of goods up-to-date. Although our income for the first year was less than $300, it grew to about $5,000 the second year, then to

$8,000 in 1956. This was almost twice as much as I had been making in the navy, and we were building up goodwill as well as our volume of business.

At the same time, the race issue was festering in our community. As the civil rights movement began to amass court victories and gain momentum in the wake of the 1954 *Brown v. Board of Education* decision, Americus, our county seat, became a stronghold of the John Birch Society. Although our actions and comments would be considered cautious and innocuous today, back then we became known as too liberal by prevailing standards. My mother was extremely outspoken, and her beliefs, shared by Rosalynn and me, were well known in the community. Although most local merchants boycotted Koinonia Farm, we sold them our certified seed peanuts, and we processed their seed in our shelling plant. Also, as a member of the Board of Education, I did everything possible to guarantee equal services to the Koinonia students in the public school system.

At that time, Georgia's top political leaders were promoting membership in White Citizens' Councils, whose stated purpose was to protect the rights of white citizens by openly opposing court-ordered desegregation. In each Georgia community, large or small, white men signed up for membership, with their five-dollar annual dues going off to some unknown destination. Our constable was the head of the organization in Plains, and he came by a couple of times to sign me up. I told him I was not interested and could tell from the cool attitude of some of our neighbors at church, Lions Club meetings, and school affairs that my rejection of the membership was well known.

My uncle Alton Carter and I had long talks about it,

and I began seriously to face the prospect of leaving Plains. Since I was one of relatively few people trained in the design and operation of the new and still highly secret nuclear power plants and had Restricted Data security clearance, I was not worried about getting a job with General Dynamics, Westinghouse, or some other company that was increasingly involved in such work. Still, I had cast my lot in Plains and wanted to stay.

One afternoon, a few days after the constable's second visit about the Citizens' Council, I looked up from sacking wheat seed to see about twenty of my best customers coming in the front door of our warehouse. The spokesman was Paul Toms, a good friend with whom I had frequently been hunting at night for raccoons and possums. Paul was embarrassed, and so was I.

He said, "Jimmy, we've come here to help with your business."

"In what way, Paul?" I asked.

He replied, "You know how much we thought of Mr. Earl, and we think almost as much of you as we did of your daddy. He was one of us, and we always knew where he stood on some of the important things."

I knew very well what he was talking about, but I asked him anyway.

"Mr. Mark says he's been to see you a couple of times about the Citizens' Council, but you don't seem to understand what it is. You're the only man in town that hasn't joined up, and we'd like to explain what we're trying to do. We're not out to hurt anybody, black or white, but we want to try to preserve our way of life."

I considered the situation for a few moments and finally said, "I know all of you are friends of my family and mean the best for us, but I don't intend to join the White Citizens' Council. This isn't the way I think we ought to go, and besides, there are a few politicians in Atlanta who are taking the dues from all over the state and putting the money in their pockets, just because folks are worried about the race issue. I've made up my mind not to do it."

One of the men said, "We heard you said the same thing when Mr. Mark came around, so we've got the five dollars here to pay your dues."

This was a new development, which pushed me into a corner. I finally got desperate, or mad, for I abandoned the polite approach, got a five-dollar bill out of the cash register, and said, "I'll take this and flush it down the toilet, but I am not going to join the White Citizens' Council."

The group made some comments about being sorry about my attitude as they left. We lost quite a few customers for several months, but eventually most of them came back.

★ ★ ★

Because of intimidation by White Citizens' Councils and the inflammatory rhetoric of politicians, the federal courts' civil rights decisions had little impact on the lives of most Georgians. Schools, churches, and most public facilities remained segregated. Although a scattering of black citizens registered to vote, this simple act of citizenship was an extraordinary event in some of the rural counties and required a lot of courage.

Our family had a close friend named Willis Wright, a

fine man who owned a farm in nearby Webster County that he had bought from my father. Although not a vocal activist, Willis was an intelligent, informed, and quietly determined man. He and I had long conversations about politics and civil rights when he came to our warehouse on business or when I stopped by his home while visiting our adjacent farm. In 1960, he became the first black citizen in Webster County to go to the courthouse to register to vote. The registrar looked at him for quite a while and then brought out a copy of the infamous thirty questions that had been imposed by the Georgia General Assembly in 1958 to screen voters. Whites were spared this ordeal, but any blacks who dared apply to vote could be deterred by a voter registrar who decided to enforce the law rigidly. We all knew that few political scientists could answer the tricky questions, such as "What is the definition of a felony in Georgia?" and "What do the constitutions of the United States and Georgia provide regarding the suspension of the writ of habeas corpus?" Blacks' answers had to agree with those of the local registrar. Willis said, "I was told that these questions are no longer required in America, and that black people now have a right to vote." Then the registrar pulled a large pistol from a drawer, laid it on the counter pointing at Willis, and said, "Nigger, you better think this over for a few more days, then let me know what you decide."

Willis immediately drove over to my warehouse office and told me what had happened. I asked him if he wanted me to go with him to the courthouse, and he said that he'd rather take care of this by himself, that it wouldn't mean much if I was there. We finally agreed that he would return and let the registrar know that he had talked to me and that I'd told him to go back and register. Willis did this without any problem, and there were no efforts to harass him. But, despite some small successes of this kind, these were still bad times in Georgia.

The entrenched county unit system excluded Negroes from playing a significant role in elections and perpetuated the political power of a relatively small portion of Georgia's voters and Democratic party politicians. There were two formidable obstacles for a potential black voter to surmount: carefully contrived state laws, the key ones embedded in the state constitution; and additional policies and rules of the Democratic party. Personal intimidation was effective in the more conservative rural areas, and the black and more liberal white voters in cities were simply robbed of voting power by the old 3-2-1 formula.

But the most effective legal pressures for change came from white Democrats who were themselves deprived of justice in a system that was supposed to be fair and democratic. It was not uncommon for one Democratic candidate to receive a majority of popular votes while his opponent won the election by having more county unit votes, as Gene Talmadge had done in 1946. In 1954, for instance, Rosalynn and I had participated in our first gubernatorial campaign after our return to Georgia and met several of the candidates who came to a large political rally in Plains. We finally decided to support different candidates. I voted for former Speaker of the House Fred Hand from Camilla, primarily because my grandfather had worked with his father in the timber and turpentine business late in the nineteenth century. I had enjoyed talking to him about this

shared family history and promised to support him. Rosalynn voted for a relatively progressive attorney, Charlie
Gowan, from Brunswick. However, Marvin Griffin, the
segregationist candidate, was elected governor with the required clear majority of county unit votes but only 36 percent of the popular votes.

The county unit system and other imbalanced voting
systems were repeatedly challenged across the nation, both
with proposed amendments to state constitutions and in the
federal courts, but without success. Most of the cases were
brought seeking equal protection of rights under the Fourteenth Amendment, to have voting power mirror more accurately the population of their communities. However,
the federal courts ruled consistently against such challenges, mostly because of an expressed aversion to usurping
the sovereign right of states to run their elections and an
even stronger reluctance to get involved in the "political
thicket" of primary elections. On appeal, the Supreme
Court of the United States, with few dissenting votes, repeatedly refused to reverse these lower court decisions.

Finally, a legal challenge was mounted that would
shake the foundation of the ancient political order. On
March 26, 1962, in *Baker v. Carr*, the U.S. Supreme Court
struck down practices throughout the United States that
permitted gross political inequities among both individual
citizens and communities. For the first time, the justices
entered the political thicket by reversing a lower court decision and declaring that there had been "invidious discrimination" against the Tennessee voters who had brought the
suit. Furthermore, the local district court was given a direct
responsibility to assure that the Tennessee legislature be

reconstituted to honor the long-ignored state constitutional requirement that representation be reasonably based on population.

This "one man, one vote" ruling had been eagerly awaited, and federal lawsuits were filed within a few days by urban dwellers in Georgia and thirty-one other states to change laws that were discriminating against them and their neighbors. In Georgia, the plaintiffs waited less than an hour to file their carefully prepared brief in the federal courts. The first and most important lawsuit brought in Georgia after *Baker v. Carr* was against the county unit system, and a second suit was soon filed calling for reappointment of the legislature.

I didn't know it then, but the outcome of these two cases would transform the political scene in Georgia and would shape the future of my life.

chapter 2

★★★★★★★★★★★★★★★★★★★★★★★★★★★★★★★★

One Man, One Vote

Looking back to the spring of 1962, I can clearly see why the *Baker v. Carr* decision hit Georgia and other states like a bombshell. Political leaders on both sides of the issue were obsessed with the subject, as were private citizens, like the members of the Carter family, who also had an intense interest in the pending federal court decisions. Perhaps a new day was coming to Georgia, but, judging from the frustrations of the past, it was not easy to sustain much real hope.

There were some notable differences in Georgia that made the applicability of the Tennessee ruling to our state doubtful. The most significant was that there was no state constitutional provision calling for representation based on population. On the one hand, the House of Representatives in Georgia was shaped by the 3-2-1 county unit system, and it would require passage of a constitutional amendment (a time-consuming and cumbersome process) to change this formula. On the other hand, composition of the state Senate was based solely on statutes and could be modified within a few days by an act of the legislature signed by the governor.

Undaunted by these obstacles was Morris Abram, the attorney for an activist citizen named James O'Hear Sanders, who had long been awaiting an opportunity to test the county unit system in the federal courts. Abram and his clients had earlier contested the outcome of a campaign for U.S. Congress in the First District of Georgia, on the Atlantic coast. The winner had received a majority of county unit votes although his opponent had more popular votes. However, this was an ex post facto case, seeking redress of damages after the election was over. The likelihood of its being heard expeditiously or providing a basis for successful appeal to the U.S. Supreme Court was slight.

It is interesting that the issue of electing members of the U.S. Congress would not be tested at all in the 1962 cases. Each district had a committee, appointed by the incumbent congressman, that was permitted by law to decide whether their election would be by popular vote or county units. Public pressure had already convinced some of these committees to shift to a popular vote. After this happened in the Fifth District, which included Atlanta, a young candidate named Charles Weltner went on to defeat longtime incumbent Congressman James Davis by 75,758 to 61,295 votes. Under the unit system, Davis would have won 8 to

6, as he had done repeatedly in the past. United States senators, being nominated as Democratic candidates (and therefore elected) statewide, were also chosen by county units.

Now, however, there was a good opportunity to cut to the heart of Georgia's political power structure. The election that would deprive Atlanta citizens like James O'Hear Sanders of their equal voice in choosing the state's leaders was not scheduled until September 1962, almost six months in the future. This legal action was designed to prevent anticipated damage, not be a retroactive suit. Also, since the U.S. Supreme Court had mandated judicial action to carry out the *Baker v. Carr* ruling, it was quite likely that a panel of three federal judges would be formed to hear the case, bypassing the more tedious route through district courts and ensuring a direct and immediate appeal of their decision to the Supreme Court. Defendants in the case were James Gray, chairman of the state Democratic committee, and Ben Fortson, secretary of state, along with other top officials in both the party and state government. This lawsuit, known as *Sanders v. Gray*, would test the legality of Georgia's laws and ancient customs that had protected rural dominance and maintained white supremacy.

It was customary in cases like this for the senior court of appeals judge, in this case Elbert P. Tuttle, to chair the panel, selecting the federal district judge to whom the original case had been submitted plus another appellate judge to join him. The litigants had filed their suit in the North Georgia District with Judge Frank A. Hooper, who had a moderate record on racial issues. Within a few days, on

April 2, 1962, Judge Tuttle named a panel consisting of himself, Judge Hooper, and a freshman court of appeals judge, Griffin Bell. Judge Bell, a distant cousin of Rosalynn's, was from Americus and had been Georgia state chairman for John F. Kennedy's highly successful 1960 presidential campaign. This was, of course, one reason that Judge Bell had been appointed to the court by President Kennedy.

Griffin Bell was but one of the key players in this story who were related to me or Rosalynn. It is sometimes difficult for non-Southerners to understand how stable the population of rural Southern communities had been since European settlers moved into these areas five or six generations earlier. The majority of our family members were direct descendants of these pioneers, mostly from England, Scotland, and Ireland, and the intermarriages and blood kinships in the neighboring towns were extensive and intricate. Rosalynn was one of the few female residents in Plains who was not related to me, at least within the last 120 years or so. Later, when Sam Nunn was elected to the U.S. Senate during my term as governor, the *Atlanta Journal* ran a front-page article describing how his grandfather and my grandmother were first cousins.

Two days after *Sanders v. Gray* was filed, a second case, *Toombs v. Fortson*, was brought by a group of citizens against Secretary of State Ben Fortson and other officials calling for reapportionment of the Georgia General Assembly on the basis of population. The two cases were intimately related, because the number of House members was tied to the number of unit votes the county had in elections. The disparity was almost ludicrous, giving a vote in the smallest counties, like Echols and Quitman, ninety-nine times as much weight in elections and legislation as that of a voter in Fulton, our largest county.

Judge Tuttle again chose Griffin Bell to join him, and District Judge Lewis R. Morgan completed the three-judge panel. There was a lot of speculation about how the four judges making up the two panels would rule. Raised in Hawaii and California, Tuttle had moved to Georgia as a young man and later became chairman of the state's tiny Republican party. After serving as general counsel for the U.S. Treasury Department, he was appointed to the federal court by President Eisenhower in 1953. He was already one of our family's heroes, having first outlawed segregation on buses in our state and then reversed a lower court ruling that barred integration of the University of Georgia.

The two district court judges, Hooper and Morgan, were Georgians who had grown up and held office under the county unit system, but the suits had been filed with them because these judges' previous decisions had pleased the plaintiffs. They had carefully avoided judges like Robert Elliott, who presided over the southwestern Georgia area that included Plains. He was a strong segregationist, and his rulings were known to represent this view.

The biggest unknown was Griffin Bell. He was a conservative who prior to his appointment had been the chief trial lawyer in a prestigious and politically active law firm. In this case, his former firm was defending the status quo.

✳ ✳ ✳

Governor Ernest Vandiver was in Europe on a trade mission when the *Baker v. Carr* ruling was announced and

Sanders v. Gray was filed. He was cautious in his comments but consistently reminded Georgians of his oath to preserve the county unit system. Other politicians were not so reticent. Herman Talmadge, now a U.S. senator, issued this first of his many pontifical statements in Washington:

> For the U.S. Supreme Court to hold that the inaction of a state legislature on the question of apportionment is a litigable question is in direct violation of the constitutional doctrine of separation of powers, upon which our republican form of government is based. With three separate, independent and coordinate branches of government . . . it is beyond the comprehension of anyone who ever has been exposed to a law book how a court at any level could compel a state legislature to take or not to take action on any question.

Former governor Marvin Griffin, who was running once again, called on his fellow citizens "to join me in opposing this nefarious scheme of these plotters who are attempting to wrest from them the control of the Democratic party." He went on, "The Atlanta newspapers are renewing their brainwashing tactics in the attempt to confuse, mislead and deceive the people of Georgia concerning the county unit system. . . . [The litigants are] fluttering around like chickens with their heads cut off but they are destined for the pot." Democratic party Chairman James Gray, the chief defendant, said, "I don't know what's going to happen. I don't see how a federal court could force the legislature into changing. If the legislators turn around and say 'no,' what could the federal court do?"

While these and hundreds of similar statements were flooding the print pages and airwaves of our state, there was a heated debate in Atlanta about whether the governor should call a special session of the legislature to accept or reject the court ruling on the county unit system, which was expected near the end of April. There was practically no sentiment among top officials to make substantive changes in the county unit system or to reapportion the legislature; they were willing to make only minimal adjustments that might satisfy the court. The conservative legislators wanted, above all, to retain the relative power of the rural areas, where their primary constituency lay and where county bosses could trade unit votes for jobs, new highways, state parks, or other goodies from the state treasury. Potential candidates for statewide office who were more progressive could see clearly that their chances would improve if voting strength could be shifted toward the big towns and cities, but they were playing the debate game on both sides so as not to irritate rural voters in case their power was preserved.

The decision to call a special session was forced by the judges' announcement that they would reapportion the legislature themselves if the state solons were unable to do so by the twenty-seventh of the month. When the members of the General Assembly came together on April 16, Governor Vandiver in his usual grandiloquent style traced the sweeping path of history to our state from ancient times through the earlier state capitals: "the tribes of Moses' day to ancient Athens, Sparta, Rome, and Carthage . . . to the

plain of Runnymede . . . to the Tower of London . . .
thence across an uncharted sea to an uncarved wilder-
ness . . . thence to Savannah . . . to Louisville . . . to
Milledgeville . . . then to Atlanta," and now to the assembled legislature, where history was again being made.
There followed a spate of proposals, with the governor's
being preeminent and constantly changing, as he accepted
ideas and compromised with political forces whose votes he
needed to prevail in the House of Representatives. The
final legislation was shaped by this negotiating procedure.
However, even the most radical proposals from these incumbent politicians retained two unit votes for each of the
121 smallest counties.

The upcoming statewide elections in September were
another factor affecting the legislative debate. The Senate
was controlled, after a fashion, by two ambitious men—its
presiding officer, Lieutenant Governor Garland Byrd, and
a competitor, President Pro Tem Carl Sanders. Byrd, a
conservative, was an announced candidate for governor,
prepared to run against Marvin Griffin. Sanders, a moderate and apparent favorite of the Atlanta newspapers, had
been running for lieutenant governor but now began to
indicate a desire to raise his sights to the state's highest
office.

Some of the metaphors and evasive phrases indicated
how politicians were reaching for new ideas without irritat-
ing voters. A senator from De Kalb County was apparently
thinking about carving his initials on live trees when he
said, "There's no need in trying to carve on dead wood."
Carl Sanders, a city slicker, had farm life on his mind: "The
legislature had better move to shut the barn door before all

of the cows and units run out," and, a few days later, "The time to act is when the horse is in the barn." Congressman J. L. Pilcher, when pushed to make an analysis, bravely expounded, "I will abide by the decision of the legislature. I'm with the people of Georgia right on!"

There were frequent efforts by the segregationists to tie the county unit and reapportionment cases to the race issue. Representative John Sheffield, former governor Griffin's floor leader and a candidate for lieutenant governor, was quite explicit. "The objective of the Atlanta manipulators," he said, "is to take over the Democratic party in Georgia and put candidates in a compromising position on segregation. When this is accomplished, they can begin to fulfill their obligations to the NAACP bloc vote. This is a sellout which, if accomplished, will trade the rural vote for the bloc vote. Personally, I like the Old Guard in Georgia that knows we are at the crossroads and will speak out against integration and will fight the NAACP in its efforts to control the Democratic party." Attorney General Eugene Cook was more subtle but just as clearly understood when he said, "I would say that Chief Justice Earl Warren prepared that case. It encompasses everything the chief justice would like to see accomplished in the Southeastern states."

Georgia quickly became divided in many ways. People and groups took positions depending on where their best interests might lie. County officials, with the exception of a few in urban areas, were committed to the county unit system, while municipal leaders were inclined to seek ways to escape the discrimination that had been foisted on those representing all except the smallest towns. Among the announced candidates for governor, Marvin Griffin was in favor of reapportioning the legislature according to population, a strangely liberal position for him. In exchange, he wanted to preserve the county unit system at all costs for statewide elections so that he could be elected governor again. Carl Sanders stayed cautious to the end and still equivocal about which higher office to seek, offering changing plans that were almost indistinguishable from those of Governor Vandiver. Lieutenant Governor Byrd prepared a proposal that likely would have met the minimum conditions of the federal judges, with a much larger legislative body that would keep a legislator for each small county while adding many seats for the medium-sized and large ones.

Some of the judges' statements indicated clearly that, for the time being, equal representation in either of the two houses of the General Assembly would be adequate in the reapportionment suit. Strangely, this option was not at first given any prominence. Perhaps this was because proponents of change considered the House so closely tied to the county unit system that most of them just ignored the Senate. Or perhaps the defendants hoped they could delay the effect of a decision, because the House composition could be modified only by a constitutional amendment, a process that might take as long as two and a half years.

In a preliminary session on April 15, the judges had made it clear that their final hearing would be on April 27, to assess whatever action the legislature might take, and that a decision would be made as quickly as possible. Perhaps sensing that the federal court was going to strike down the county unit system and throw the statewide races wide open, Carl Sanders now announced that he would be a candidate for governor against Marvin Griffin and Garland Byrd.

More than two dozen bills had been introduced in the special session to deal with the court ruling. These proposals were given descriptive names, including the "Render Hill Twist," "George L. Smith Polka," and "Roy Harris Shift." The final choice boiled down to the governor's more conservative bill, which had passed 147–37 in the House, and the lieutenant governor's, adopted 41–7 in the Senate. To indicate the complexity of the legislative maneuvering, the House compromise was a substitute for a substitute for a substitute for a substitute.

This bill called for every county, regardless of size, to have two unit votes, plus one more for each 15,000 people. A candidate who got a clear majority of popular votes would receive all the county's unit votes; if no candidate won a majority, the unit votes for the county would be prorated according to the proportion of popular votes received. On a statewide basis, a candidate who won a majority of both popular and unit votes would win; otherwise there would be a runoff between the two top candidates, with the second election determined on the basis of unit votes. Although there were a few other subtle differences between the House and Senate versions, the most important Senate provision was that in the first election all unit votes in each county would be allocated in the same proportion as the popular vote. This feature was designed to reduce chances of "bloc" voting (that is, black voting) in the larger urban counties. The General Assembly and Governor Vandiver were still clinging desperately to the county unit system.

There was a lot of sparring between the two legislative bodies. After hearing three young women sing a few songs during a respite in the debates, Representative Robert Andrews of Gainesville rose on a point of order and said, "I move that these beautiful young ladies now go over to Mocking Bird Hill across the way and sing to them, 'We've Got Plenty of Nothing' and wind up by singing 'The Lieutenant Governor Is Standing on the Corner Watching All the Votes Go By.' "

Eventually, the House and Senate conference committee met and deadlocked, while the governor attempted to focus either encouragement or ridicule on the legislators for their failure to make a decision. Finally, the House met, voted for its own plan, and adjourned. The Senate was then faced with either accepting the House version or being blamed for turning the whole decision over to the federal judges. They chose the first option but, to demonstrate their anger, refused to adjourn. Vandiver signed the bill and sent a copy over to the federal judges. For the first time in Georgia's history, the governor had to issue an executive order dissolving the General Assembly.

The *Sanders v. Gray* judicial panel was already in session, waiting to receive the legislature's bill as soon as it could be hand-delivered. The judges permitted the plaintiffs and defendants to analyze the *Baker v. Carr* decision. The key word in the decisions in this county unit case and in the reapportionment case would be *invidious*. In effect, the Supreme Court had said in *Baker v. Carr* that some discrimination against urban voters was permissible but that "invidious inequality" would have to be corrected by the lower courts. Like thousands of Georgians, Rosalynn and I got out our dictionary to look up the word, which implied things such as "causing envy, discontent, discomfort, harm, or resentment." Chief Defense Attorney Buck Murphy tried to call attention to the ambiguities surrounding this definition, telling the panel, "I don't know what 'invidious discrimination' is."

"We have to decide, unfortunately," responded Judge Tuttle, and the judges sought detailed analysis of the new legislation.

A Georgia State University professor testified. He had calculated that 51 percent of the population had 45 percent of the unit votes when the current county unit law went into effect in 1917. Under the bill just passed, the same population percentage would only have 33 percent of the unit votes. The plaintiffs also described the abuse of election laws that had become acceptable under the county bosses. Long County, for instance, had 160 percent as many registered voters as the eligible population, voters exceeded adults in Union County by 42 percent and in Franklin County by 47 percent. All this despite the fact that all black citizens were counted as eligible even though few of them had been permitted to register. Murphy was so bold as to defend these inequities by stating, "I think the legislature has got a right to diffuse political strength."

The next day, April 28, the panel announced its decision. Judge Bell read the opinion aloud, much as is done by the Supreme Court in rendering important decisions. The judges unanimously declared that the county unit system was invalid "in its present form" and forbade its use in the September 12 Democratic primary or future elections. This was one of the most momentous political decision of the century in Georgia, almost surely requiring the governor and other statewide officers henceforth to be chosen in statewide elections, with each vote being given equal weight regardless of where the voter lived. Fulton County would now have 14.1 percent of the votes, compared with 7.3 percent under the legislature's bill and 1.5 percent under the existing system. Echols and Quitman counties, the state's two smallest, would face a commensurate reduction in political power. Judge Bell later recalled that the *Sanders v. Gray* decision "was not a shock to the political establishment. The decision was more like the funeral of someone who had passed away after a long illness. The prevailing thought of many who had profited from the system seemed to be that it was well while it lasted. The new day was coming, but it had not yet taken form."

The new shape of Georgia politics became more apparent less than a month later, on May 25, when the panel in *Toombs v. Fortson* held that the apportionment of both houses in the state legislature maintained "invidious discrimination" between rural and urban voters. Judge Tuttle, writing for the court, ordered that at least one house be reapportioned according to population by 1963. If the legislature failed to act, the federal courts would establish the districts.

✵ ✵ ✵

Like other Georgia citizens, Rosalynn, my mother, and I followed these legislative debates and court proceedings with great attention. This was the major news item to be read and discussed at our peanut warehouse, at church, at Lions Club meetings, and in the small county newspapers. The system was so firmly entrenched that we had never really considered the possibility or advisability of its being changed. Now, to hear all the horror stories about voting inequities was surprising. Our own county, Sumter, was one of the middle-sized ones, and we had never felt particularly benefited or deprived by the county unit arrangement. Although the main struggle was for political power, it was the race issue that was most discussed. An oversimplification was the question: How might our lives be changed if the people in Atlanta make the political decisions in the future? More personally, many people believed they now faced what racist leaders had long predicted: the disruption of religious worship, the end of public education for white students, and numerous interracial marriages.

My own interest in the legislature's action was becoming much more intense. Although fully occupied with our family business and my many other community responsibilities, I remained interested in politics. As a member and then chairman of the Sumter County Board of Education, I was embarrassed by the condition of our state's public school system. Under the "separate but equal" provision of the U.S. Supreme Court's 1896 *Plessy v. Ferguson* ruling, the "separate" was the only part honored in the South. There was certainly no equality between black and white students.

When I became a member of the board, my seasoned colleagues and I decided to visit all the schools in the county. There were two high schools and three grammar schools for white students, and it was natural that we visit these first. We found them to be in fairly good condition, although the buildings were pre-1930s vintage. Buses served all the rural homes, books were adequate and current, and there were numerous extracurricular activities in sports, drama, extemporaneous writing, and debating.

Then we began visiting the county schools for black children. There were twenty-six of them for the elementary grades, a few of which also served high school students. There were so many sites because no buses were provided, and schools had to be within walking distance of the children's homes. The books were those that had been declared too worn out for use in the white schools. Classes were held in various places, including Sunday school classrooms of black churches and even private homes. For some reason, my most vivid memory is of large teenage boys trying to sit on chairs designed for children of kindergarten age. After a few of these embarrassing visits, my fellow board members and I found various reasons not to go on any others.

This was before Head Start and other compensatory programs of the Great Society years, and when the South felt confident that the federal courts would not interfere in decisions made by local education officials. All school board members were, of course, white community leaders similar to those who served at the state level, chosen in the all-white Democratic primaries, appointed by segregationist governors or voted in, as I was, by county grand juries on which black citizens rarely if ever served. The South was hunkered down during the late 1950s and early 1960s, fearful of civil rights threats but confident that desegregation could be postponed almost indefinitely. There were spotted instances of new buildings being constructed for all-black schools, to strengthen the separate but equal claim, and eventually the state authorities did add some school buses to serve the black community (on which both front fenders of the otherwise all-yellow buses were painted black).

Without doing anything heroic or economically suicidal, we school board members tried in every way possible to improve the county's school system, for children of both races. We had observed with great interest the *Brown v. Board of Education* ruling but had then seen Congress repeatedly defeat or remove enforcement provisions from civil rights legislation that would have made the judicial decision effective in Georgia. During those days, Southern governors like Orval Faubus in Arkansas, Ross Barnett in Mississippi, and George Wallace in Alabama became famous by defying federal court orders and encouraging their supporters to confront federal troops sent in to enforce the law. To our state's credit, none of the officials of Georgia's 200 public school districts or any state officer ever took similar action.

This did not mean, however, that Georgians were supporting the admission of black students to the all-white schools. Our senior U.S. senator, Richard Russell, was the undisputed leader of the Southern segregationist forces, and he was not shy about using his immense prestige, power, and political wiles to thwart efforts to pass federal civil rights legislation. On eleven occasions, beginning in 1938, he had led successful efforts to block passage of such laws. As mentioned earlier, our relatively progressive Governor Ernest Vandiver had been elected in 1958 on his pledge of "No, not one!" Even Ralph McGill, the liberal editor of the *Atlanta Constitution* and the South's chief proponent of racial progress, made it plain that he was not in favor of racial integration but only supported equality of opportunity under the law.

Meanwhile, more concerted attempts were being made in Washington to pass far-reaching bills that would implement the *Brown* decision. President Dwight D. Eisenhower and Senate Majority Leader Lyndon B. Johnson supported major civil rights legislation in 1957 and again in 1960, but their efforts proved fruitless when House-passed legislation reached the Senate. After John F. Kennedy's election as president in 1960, many Americans expected that civil rights legislation would be pushed with new fervor. This, however, did not happen. Until his death, President Kennedy resisted the growing demands, even from Vice President Johnson, for a strong White House effort to pass laws that would integrate the public schools and guarantee voting rights to blacks and other minority citizens.

The county unit system had always been the bastion of the most ardent segregationists in Georgia. Everyone knew this, although this aspect of the court's decisions was seldom mentioned in official circles. During the judges' final hearing before rendering their decision on *Sanders v. Gray*, Morris Abram brought up discrimination against Negro voters. Judge Bell challenged him immediately for raising a completely new question. "What I want to know is what we are trying here," he said. "You seem to be trying to inject the Fifteenth Amendment of the U.S. Constitution," which prohibits disfranchisement of voters on the basis of race. Abram immediately backed off, replying, "We're trying the Fourteenth and Seventeenth amendments only," which deal with equal protection of the law and the direct election of U.S. senators.

Now, with the panel's ruling, the county unit system was gone, and the state government would have to reapportion at least one house of the General Assembly strictly on the basis of population. The federal judges had delayed their next decisions to allow the state to hold the primary for governor and other state officials using direct popular elections before the reapportionment decision would have to be made. This meant that the aftermath of the ruling was a brief period of relative quiet, as exhausted legislators went home to rest and all government leaders tried to decide what to do next. Hearings were convened by a special study committee set up by House resolution, but the Senate refused to participate. Early in May, Lieutenant Governor Byrd suffered a mild heart attack and withdrew from the governor's race, leaving a contest between Carl Sanders and Marvin Griffin.

Attention soon focused almost exclusively on the primary election campaigns that were permitted. These included races for statewide office and for the General Assembly, although the future status of those nominated for the legislature was still uncertain. Those who aspired to sit in the House of Representatives ran in their home counties, but the situation for prospective state senators was more complicated. Fulton County (Atlanta) had its own senator, and Chatham (Savannah) and Effingham shared one. All the other Senate districts consisted of three counties, regardless of size. These rotated every two years in choosing a senator to represent the entire district, with only a plurality of votes in the home county required for election. Of the fifty-four Senate seats, twenty-four had already been filled by Democratic nominees under the county rotation system.

Since senators could serve only one two-year term, Senate seats had no long-term political value. Either a popular House member would decide to serve for one term in the smaller Senate and then return to his House seat or a prestigious nonpolitician would run for the honor of the job. Often there was no opposition. Furthermore, since voters in Georgia's smallest counties could elect a senator during their time in the rotation, routinely one of the fifty-four members would represent less than one-twentieth of 1 percent of the state's population. For instance, beginning in 1917 Dr. Loren Gary of Quitman County was repeatedly elected to the House of Representatives by about 500 voters, except when he decided on several occasions to serve in the Senate. When he died in office in 1949, his son Britt finished out his Senate term and then was elected to the House without a break in the family's service.

Although a rash of proposals involving both houses of the legislature was put forward to comply with the reapportionment opinion, attention was beginning to shift toward the Senate. Although the current system had remained intact since 1877, the size and composition of the Senate could be changed expeditiously by a legislative act. Also, there were 205 House members with seniority, while the 54 Senators were prevented from building up tenure by the three-county rotation system.

About a week before the Democratic primary, the judges responded to some questions that had been proposed to the court by plaintiffs in the reapportionment case. In effect, they advised that the Senate be the reconstituted chamber. The districts would have to be approximately equal in population, with only one senator for each, and the Democratic nominees could be chosen only by the voters in "meaningful elections" and not in district conventions. The judges also announced that they would reconvene the second week in October to assess the state government's progress in carrying out their order.

In the September 12 gubernatorial primary, Carl Sanders won the Democratic nomination, and would have no significant Republican opposition. Sanders had conducted a modern media-based campaign, while Marvin Griffin had run with an outdated platform and campaign style. His old-fashioned political rallies attracted large crowds, who came to eat and listen to the candidate's biting and folksy humor. Griffin received about the same popular vote as in 1954, less than 40 percent, but the county unit system was no longer there to save him. His comment was "The folks ate my barbecue but voted the other way."

Sanders announced immediately that he would cooperate with Governor Vandiver and legislative leaders in reapportioning the Senate, and, after some consultation, the governor called a special session for this purpose to convene on September 27.

✷ ✷ ✷

Over the years, I had been encouraged to run for office by a few of my neighbors and others with whom I had worked on civic affairs. However, we had a growing family, and I was deeply immersed in our expanding business. I was already devoting a large portion of my time to public projects, which I enjoyed, and felt satisfied with my position in the community. By this time I was chairman of the county school board, was a member of the local hospital authority, had led the formation of a seven-county planning commission and a similar state organization and was chairman of both, was president of the Georgia Crop Improvement Association (responsible for all varieties of seed used in our state), was active in our church, and was a leader in the Lions Clubs of the state. I had a good and full life and, in comparison, being one of 205 members of the state House of Representatives or a rotating senator did not appeal to me. I had given some private thoughts to running for the U.S. Congress but did not relish moving to Washington on a full-time basis.

However, the proposed new Georgia Senate was more attractive. It would likely be completely reconstituted, have increasing influence and authority, and provide an opportunity for reelection and the accumulation of seniority. At the same time, the regular legislative sessions in our state were restricted by the constitution to a limited number of working days each year during January, February, and March, when our warehouse business would be least demanding on my time. We would just be shelling peanuts, breaking land on our farms, spreading lime on our customers' fields, and applying nitrogen topdressing on winter grain.

In my school board work I had become increasingly frustrated with the policies imposed on us by the state government, and I could envision playing a role in shaping legislative and budget decisions in Atlanta that could help the public school system in Sumter County. It seemed likely also that, with the county unit system struck down and with Carl Sanders as our next governor, there was the prospect of a more enlightened environment in dealing with racial issues. All the Carter family had voted for Sanders, but we thought he had gone a little far when he referred to his supporters as the "law-abiding, God-fearing, sound-thinking people of Georgia," who had defeated the "forces of disunity, discord, and dishonor."

I wanted to keep my options open and, uncharacteristically, did not even mention these thoughts about running for the Senate to Rosalynn or anyone else. September was peanut and cotton harvesttime, and I had to monitor very closely the maintenance of purity as we gathered seed peanuts, which had become the primary interest of our business. In addition, we purchased several thousand tons of peanuts from farmers in our area, most of which would later be shelled and resold for use as salted nuts, in candy, and as peanut butter. This was also the only time we had for collection of debts owed to us by farmers for the seed, fertilizer, and pesticides that we had sold them on credit earlier in the year.

During this period we worked around the clock, buying and processing peanuts and ginning cotton. When they weren't in school, our three boys worked long hours with Rosalynn and me. For days at a time, we took naps and ate all our meals at the warehouse and only went home for a brief shower every day or so. It was an incredibly busy season, during which we earned most of our annual income. There was little time left for starting a new political career, and I was afraid that even to broach such a subject at that time might precipitate a well-justified family revolution.

When the General Assembly convened for the special session on September 27, Governor-nominee Sanders, who was still serving as Senate president pro tem, was riding a crest of popularity and power, and there was little doubt that the reapportionment plan he endorsed would be passed in its general form. It called for the fifty-four Senate nominees to be chosen by majority vote in a special Democratic primary October 16 and routinely confirmed by the state Democratic convention the following day. Necessary runoff elections would be held on October 23. Then these nominees would face possible Republican opponents, with the victors officially elected in the regularly scheduled general election on November 6. The average district would include about 70,000 citizens, but the judges permitted deviations of up to 20 percent from this figure, roughly equivalent to the disparity among the fifty states in the electoral college for choosing the president of the United States. Only one of the existing three-county districts in the state would likely be unchanged, because it just happened to have almost exactly one fifty-fourth of the state's population. In general terms it sounded simple, but the devil was in the details concerning the other fifty-three districts.

Any reapportionment session can be an ugly and unpleasant experience for legislators. So many issues that usually lurk beneath the surface of everyday politics force themselves into the debate: race, rural-urban balance, county affiliations, family and personal friendships, the honoring of county lines, relative strengths of adjacent incumbents, and many other factors have to be considered. Each change made in one district's boundaries obviously affects the adjacent districts, creating a chain reaction that continues across the state like tumbling dominoes. Special consideration always has to be given to the interests of the more powerful legislative leaders. In the 1962 reapportionment, many of the fifty-four men who had already been nominated to Senate seats under the old rotating system became fervent lobbyists in the halls of the state capitol, attempting to preserve what they now considered to be rightfully theirs.

Although it was obvious from the beginning that Carl Sanders could get his preference through the Senate, the plan stirred up a hornet's nest in the House, which was proud of its own prerogatives. One of the House leaders dismissively told a reporter, "We haven't found anyone over here who supports the Senate bill." The representatives who were most concerned with their own county's placement spent a lot of time over in the Senate trying to help shape the decisions being made there, because this was the version that would have the imprimatur of the incoming governor. As the Senate Rules Committee neared the end of its deliberations, there were heated exchanges, allegations (all true) of vote swapping, and numerous shifts of district boundaries.

The last decision made by the Senate before voting on the final bill affected the new Fourteenth District, which included our home county of Sumter. Quitman County, on the western boundary of Georgia and directly across the Chattahoochee River from Eufaula, Alabama, was moved from the Eleventh District into the Fourteenth. This change was sought by Joe Hurst, the representative from Quitman County, and by Homer Moore, a businessman from Richland who had already defeated three other candidates in Stewart County to gain the senatorial nomination for the old three-county district that included Quitman. Hurst was recognized as the real power in the county, so it was not of much significance that incumbent Senator Robert McKenzie from Quitman County disapproved of this change, preferring to be in the more southern district along the banks of the river, where he had more friends and potential support for reelection. Since this was such a small county, with a total population of only 2,400, it made little difference in the size of either district. On October 1, the Senate approved the transfer of Quitman County and ratified the reapportionment bill by a vote of 43 to 9.

Now, in the relative quiet of our state capitol, it was up to the House of Representatives to complete the task of reapportionment. Despite some minor shuffling of counties, there were no substantive changes in the Senate bill. It was passed, the discrepancies ironed out, and the bill was signed into law on October 5. Under its provisions, candidates would have to qualify before 5:00 P.M. on October 8, and the election would be held just eight days later. There were no further changes in our Fourteenth Senatorial District.

I didn't have any particular interest in Quitman County, or where it might wind up. I had already made my decision to run.

chapter 3

✶✶✶✶✶✶✶✶✶✶✶✶✶✶✶✶✶✶✶✶✶✶✶✶✶✶✶✶✶✶

My First
Campaign

While I was at the U.S. Naval Academy and later on ships, my duties took me to Washington every now and then, and I always visited our Georgia Congressman Carl Vinson, who was chairman of the House Committee on Naval Affairs, and the Senate chambers where Senators Walter F. George and Richard B. Russell served. Senator Russell, as chairman of the Armed Services Committee, was especially interested in the navy's new programs, which, on a few occasions, I had a chance to discuss with him. After I joined the nuclear submarine program, I went to Washington more frequently to meet with my boss, Admiral Hyman Rickover. All of us had watched the political developments closely in 1952, when Admiral Rickover was almost forced out of the navy by conservative senior officers and was saved only by the strong actions of President Harry Truman and congressional leaders, including my fellow Georgians.

Despite my interest in political affairs, any direct involvement in partisan politics was strongly discouraged among naval officers. On one occasion, in 1948, while our ship was anchored in Norfolk harbor, Henry Wallace came to speak in the community. I decided to go hear what he had to say. One of my jobs was to be aide to the executive officer, a Commander Smythe, and I mentioned my plans to him. He looked at me sternly and asked, "Are you prepared to give up your career in the navy?" I stammered and assured him that I had no such intention. "Then stay away from political meetings," he said. For this and other reasons, my contacts with political life were transient and superficial while I was in the navy, although I was a firmly committed, and somewhat lonely, Democrat. Later that year, after I was assigned to the submarine force and while I was undergoing training at the submarine school in New London, Connecticut, Rosalynn and I were the only couple out of fifty-one who openly supported Harry Truman against Tom Dewey.

✫ ✫ ✫

Fourteen years later, far from the navy and back home in Plains, I had decided to be a candidate myself. The strangest aspect of these political events, as I look back three decades, is that I didn't discuss my pending decision with Rosalynn. This would have been inconceivable in later years. However, the first intimation she had of my intentions was when I got up early in the morning on Monday, October 1, my thirty-eighth birthday, and began to put on my Sunday pants instead of the work clothes I always wore to the warehouse. She asked me where I was going, and I replied that I was on my way to the newspaper office in Americus to get the latest news on reapportionment of the state Senate. Unless there were unexpected changes in what had been decided, I was going to place a notice in the *Times-Recorder* that I would be a candidate. She was amazed but approved of my announcement. I got there early enough for the news story to be in the afternoon paper, a small item on the front page dominated by the headline "Two Die in Mississippi Riots." On the streets of Oxford, Mississippi, 4,000 federal troops were facing a mob who had been encouraged by Governor Ross Barnett to prevent the enrollment of James Meredith as the first black student at the University of Mississippi.

It was fifteen days before the Senate election.

I liked what I had heard about our new seven-county district. We lived in the largest county, Sumter, and most of our family farmland was in adjoining Webster County. We also had some farmer customers in both Stewart and Terrell counties. I didn't know much about Randolph or Chattahoochee, however, except that my Grandfather William Carter was buried in the former, where his family had been living when he was killed in a fight, and my mother's Gordy ancestors had lived and were buried in the latter. And as far as Quitman County was concerned, I considered it too small to be a significant factor in the overall vote. However, I thought I could do well there because Rosalynn's second cousin, Ralph Balkcom, was the county school superintendent and could help me with the local political leaders. Most of the towns in our district had Lions Clubs, usually the only men's civic organizations in the small communities. There were fifty-four of these clubs in southwestern Georgia, and, as the district governor responsible for them, I was well known by all the Lions.

We had some real concerns in our own county. There was overt animosity among segregationist leaders about the relatively liberal reputation of our family. They were true believers, vocal and well organized, while many of those who were more moderate on the race issue were equivocal enough to consider both sides of the issue and were also reluctant to express their views in public. However, from private conversations with our friends and discussions among the school board members, I could tell that more and more of our neighbors were ready to accept the federal court rulings about desegregation, in ways that would minimize any negative effect on their own families, and move on to other things.

An adverse political factor of greater importance was the unanimous decisions of the Sumter County and Americus school boards early in 1962 to consolidate the two systems and combine all the small high schools into one with a much more comprehensive program. With professional assistance from the State Department of Education, we had completed a definitive study of the pros and cons of this issue. There was little doubt that the students could have a more flexible curriculum, the academic and vocational subjects could be more tailored to suit their ultimate careers, those with different learning abilities could be taught with more individual attention, better teachers could be recruited, and administrative costs would be reduced by consolidation. Special funding was available from the state to help pay for the new buildings. We members of the school board also felt that the citizens of Americus and the rural areas would be more likely to work harmoniously in promoting economic growth if we shared a common school system.

As chairman of the Sumter County school board, I had the unpleasant duty of explaining the reasons for this proposal through the news media and in public meetings to extremely doubtful and often vituperative citizens. The counterarguments were emotional, with emphasis on how personal the instruction could be in a small group of teachers and students. Also, the opponents said, just look around the community and assess the school's graduates. Could these good people possibly have been better parents or church members, more public spirited or successful as farmers or merchants, if they had driven each day across the county to go to a large school? Furthermore, what would happen to the rural towns after the schools, athletic teams, and other activities left them?

Although most families in Americus, the county seat, were supportive, the rural folks were deeply divided. Many people in the two small towns of Plains and Leslie were bitterly opposed to any change that would move the high school out of their communities. Justifiably or not, one of their most effective arguments was that this was just another surreptitious effort to integrate black and white students. There was some truth in this allegation. If and when the schools might be integrated, a consolidated system could much better accommodate the cultural and other differences among the students.

It was an ugly political battle. My first cousin Hugh Carter, a local merchant, was the leader of the opposition, and many other families were divided on the issue. Feelings became so intense that some of our closest friends and neighbors would not speak to me or Rosalynn, even at church. I'll always remember driving up to the service station in Plains one morning, as usual, to buy gasoline and have the oil checked in my pickup truck. With a small fleet of trucks and automobiles, our family were among the station's best customers. The proprietor and his helpers sat on a bench and looked at me, but none of them moved to see what I wanted. I stayed there for a few minutes and then drove over to our warehouse, where I called one of the wholesale fuel distributors in Americus and ordered a tank to be installed for our business and personal use.

Separate referendums on school consolidation were held in Americus and outside the city limits. City residents voted three to one to approve the proposal, but it was defeated by a small margin, eighty-eight votes, in the rural part of the county. The next morning when I went down to our warehouse, there was a sign nailed across the door, COONS AND CARTERS GO TOGETHER. This was a clear indication that much of the opposition had come from the fervent segregationists. Nevertheless, there was no doubt in my mind that I had been on the right side of this issue. Taking Sumter County as a whole, a strong majority had supported the school board's proposal.

I was still school board chairman when the Senate election came, and all of us knew that school consolidation would be an important factor. It was generally assumed that the consolidation issue would be raised again whenever its supporters thought it might have a better chance of passage, and a state senator could have a lot of influence on the outcome of the next referendum. Some of my friends alleged, only partly in jest, that I was running for the Senate just to get off the school board.

There was some truth in that allegation. I had been in the midst of local education crises for almost seven years and had been discouraged by the consolidation vote. No matter how determined we were to improve the school system, it would be several years before a new referendum could be launched. Even so, my intense interest in education became the most important factor in my decision to run for the Senate. In my campaign advertisements, this was always the most prominent item. I understood the controversial issues from the bottom up, and education was a subject of great public concern. Not only was the public school system threatened by opponents of integration but there was also little opportunity for most people in southwest Georgia to complete college work. In an area of more than 25,000 square miles, with a million people, there was not a single four-year college. When our students completed their junior college work or when teachers wanted to upgrade their certificates with additional courses, they had to go either to the University of Georgia in faraway Athens or across the river to Auburn, Alabama. The out-of-state tuition fees in Alabama were more than most families could afford. We had a junior college in Americus, which I hoped to help promote to senior status.

I would be facing formidable opposition in the campaign, but I was intrigued with the issues of race and education, and the state Senate would be the best place for me to exert my influence. With something like blind faith or innocence, I just prepared to run without even talking to anyone about what might come next.

In Americus and particularly in the Leslie area, some community leaders had announced their support for Homer Moore, my opponent, even before I decided to run. Others, including those who had opposed me in the public meetings on school consolidation, immediately stated that they would work to defeat me. However, it was quite likely that what votes I might lose in the rural communities would be more than equaled by gains in Americus.

Even with some difficulties at home, I felt that the biggest problem of all would be in the western part of the district, where my opponent had such a strong base of support. I knew Homer Moore to be a formidable adversary. Forty-four years old, he was an honest, hard-driving, ambitious, and active community leader. He happened to be one of my most aggressive but friendly competitors in the farm supply business. The only significant differences in our broad-based farm supply businesses were that he also had a hardware store and I had a cotton gin and a small plant for shelling seed peanuts. Homer and I regularly visited the same farmers who lived between Plains and his hometown of Richland, eighteen miles to the west, seeking to sell them seed and fertilizer and to provide a market for their peanuts. He had qualified early in the spring as his home county's nominee under the old three-county rotating system. Only a plurality of votes was required then, and he had come in ahead of three other candidates with just one-third of the total votes cast in Stewart County. He was unopposed when the Democratic primary elections were held statewide on September 12. Homer had already announced officially that he would be a candidate in whatever district his county might be placed.

After announcing for the Senate seat, I got Rosalynn to help me design some calling cards and campaign posters. Whenever I could leave the warehouse, a few hours each day, I moved around the district trying to visit friends, peanut and cotton customers, my relatives and Rosalynn's, fellow Lions Club members, city and county officials, and other community leaders who might be willing and able to help me garner a few votes. Although everyone was polite enough, many of the more knowledgeable people were cautious in their promises of support and quizzical about my ability to win the election against an opponent who had been campaigning for several months.

I tried to make it clear that I was not running a personal campaign against Homer Moore, and that I respected him as an honest and able opponent. I knew very little about his political associates, except that most of the established and more conservative leaders were supporting him as the likely victor. By the time I realized how doubtful my victory would be, I was already committed to the race and never considered turning back. I just became more determined to make an all-out effort to win. Neither did I ever have any thought that the state Senate might be a stepping-stone to higher office; this ambition alone was stretching my imagination. The force driving me was a somewhat naive concept of public service.

Still in the midst of harvest season, both Homer and I had to be at our warehouse operations for a few hours each day, taking advantage of slack times to dash around the district asking for support, seeking favorable publicity, or responding as quickly as possible to each other's political advertisements. There was no time for doing organizational work, planning a coherent media campaign, raising campaign funds, or enunciating a political platform.

As I would understand more clearly in the coming days, some of the more devout religious leaders looked with disfavor on the entire political process. I remember that during the campaign we were having annual revival at our church, and, as one of the deacons, I was expected to attend the services each night. It is still the custom for different families to entertain the visiting preacher for dinner and supper, and on my mother's night for this duty she invited Rosalynn and me to eat with them. When we sat down, Mother's guest immediately expressed his surprise and disapproval of my decision to run for the Senate seat.

He asked, "If you want to be of service to other people, why don't you go into the ministry or some honorable social service work?"

Somewhat annoyed, I asked him, "How would you like to be the pastor of a church with eighty thousand members?"

He finally admitted that it might be possible to stay honest and still minister to the needs of almost that many citizens in the Fourteenth District.

As it turned out, one of the most discouraging aspects of this rapid campaigning was the size of the district and its sparse population. It was frustrating not to be able to reach more voters. The Fourteenth Senatorial District encompassed almost 2,000 square miles and had two dozen little communities in addition to the seven county seats. I visited all I could, plus as many of the country crossroads stores as

I could reach. My lack of experience greatly reduced the effectiveness of my efforts. On too many of my early visits I became bogged down in encounters with loafers who were almost professional raconteurs and political debaters. With not much else to do, they were experts at embroiling me in idle talk or long discussions on the more controversial issues of the day.

I soon learned to concentrate as much of my time as possible on the area's radio stations, where I would attempt to wrangle a brief conversation on the air with a lonely disc jockey. Other productive visits were to the local newspapers, where there was always the possibility of an interview or even a photograph for the upcoming edition. The only regional newspapers were those published in the city of Columbus, located on the Georgia-Alabama line north of our district. My visit there to obtain some news coverage was a total failure, although I did see an article every now and then about my opponent.

On October 8, eight days before the election, Homer and I both drove to Atlanta and paid our $500 fees to run for the Senate. In all previous elections for the state legislature, candidates had signed up at their local courthouses. Now, however, there was no time for the state officials to distribute instructions and qualification forms to the 159 counties. Another change, potentially more significant, was that in this election the winner would have to get a clear majority of the votes cast instead of the plurality that had been required in the past. The only other announced candidate in the district was Clarence Chambless, a propane gas dealer from Terrell County who, like Homer Moore, had been nominated in his old three-county district. I learned later that Chambless had already pledged his support to my opponent, a decision that the two men had delayed announcing until after qualifying day for its maximum effect. With Chambless out of contention, Homer and I would not be faced with a potential runoff election, since, barring an exact tie, one of us was sure to receive a majority of votes.

One hundred and thirty-six Democratic and sixteen Republican candidates qualified to run in the fifty-four Senate districts, but most media attention was being given to Leroy Johnson, a Democrat in one of the Atlanta districts and a favorite to be elected. He had served as county prosecutor, the first black to be appointed to such a post in the Deep South. Now he was making history again, being the first black candidate for the state legislature since Reconstruction days. It was quite a coincidence that one of the few Republicans who qualified to run outside the Atlanta area was my second cousin Perry Gordy, in Columbus, about whom I had heard but whom I had not met. Since neither of the two Democrats who qualified in the two city districts faced opposition in the primary, Perry said he just wanted to add some excitement to the general election race. He would go on to win a surprising victory.

With only a week between qualifying and voting day, it was a strange campaign. There were few opportunities for speeches, and we held no political rallies. I had no campaign organization or surrogates to represent me at public affairs. I took my few posters, a hammer, and some roofing nails with me in my car. In the approaches to towns and where some of the main roads crossed in the country, I nailed up my picture, with CARTER and SENATOR being the only two words large enough for passersby to read. A few business proprietors were willing for me to display my appeal for support, usually on an equal basis with the posters and campaign literature of Homer Moore.

It was difficult to arouse interest in the Senate race, because this would be the sixth election in Georgia in as many months (counting the runoffs) and the voters were tired of politics. Most of the other voting days had involved a wide range of offices, but a few Senate seats were the only ones now at stake. Since many of those already nominated did not have opposition, there was not much statewide news coverage of the election. We didn't expect a large turnout, so it was especially important to encourage our own folks to vote. It was too late for us to get voter lists and make calls in the entire district as Homer had been able to do, but we did get the list for Sumter County.

As much as possible during the busy harvest season, my family helped in the campaign. Rosalynn, my mother, and my sister Gloria tried to make as many telephone calls as possible on one of our two warehouse lines. If they found someone who offered to help, the new volunteer was asked to take a portion of the voter list for similar calls.

Rosalynn did yeoman's work with those phone lists. Even decades later her memories are vivid:

"In my spare time I tried to call everyone on the voters list in Sumter County. It was sheer drudgery calling one number after another, and my ear got sore and my mouth hurt from talking. But I kept calling and soon I had help. Jimmy's sister Gloria and I, along with other friends, addressed thousands of letters and divided the voters list for other volunteers to call. I took one afternoon off and went door to door, to every house in Plains, to tell people that Jimmy was going to run for the Senate, asking them to vote for him. It was difficult at first, because I knew many of the people hadn't supported us on the school issue, but they were all courteous. One said, 'What in the world is Jimmy Carter going to do next?' "

✷ ✷ ✷

We were all amateurs, never having been in the inner circle of a candidate's supporters or advisers. The school referendum had been our most personal involvement in an election. But my most pervasive memory of the campaign itself is its brevity; I still find it surprising how few days were available to us to mount support.

Homer came into the campaign with some substantial advantages. Although he could not have known the exact delineation of the district except during the last few days of the legislative session, he had spent a lot of time in Atlanta when the districts were being put together. His campaign manager, State Representative Sam Singer, also from Stewart County, was an experienced political operator, and he had been helping satisfy Homer's preferences as decisions were made. They had a good organization, knew the members of the legislature in the counties around his, and had calling cards and literature already printed and distributed. Homer began campaigning aggressively in each of the counties as soon as he learned it would be in the Fourteenth District, even before Quitman County—one of his original three counties—was added at the last minute.

In his brochures, advertising, and public statements, Homer hammered repeatedly on the claim that he had already been elected "fair and square" and that the federal courts should not be permitted to undo what the people of the district had done. Although not a defensible statement in this totally different senatorial district, it proved to be very effective. It was the basis of the most frequent question I heard when I visited newspaper offices or radio stations or when I approached people to ask for their support.

The best way for either of us to reach potential supporters was through radio and newspaper advertisements. Our radio ads were usually just reading aloud the newspaper text. It should be remembered that, except for the daily *Americus Times-Recorder*, there were just the two weekly newspapers in the district—the *Dawson News* and the *Stewart-Webster Journal*. After my first announcement, published in both papers on October 4, I could only run an advertisement one time, the following week, before the election on October 16. Our advertising contest was confined to the last few days of the campaign, mostly in the *Times-Recorder* and on the radio stations in Americus and Dawson. This statement was printed up on Homer Moore's campaign sheets and was run in every newspaper edition, beginning on October 12:

TO THE VOTERS
OF SUMTER COUNTY:

This is directed to those who believe in fair play and sportsmanship.

Homer Moore of Stewart County was elected to the State Senate in a long, hard, expensive campaign. Before serving a day, he is being forced to run again because of reapportionment.

Mr. Moore's three counties of Webster, Stewart, and Quitman were left intact in the new 14th Senatorial District. Sumter County was lifted away from its old counties and added to the counties in Mr. Moore's district. Sumter County is a new sister in the above group. Thinking citizens of Sumter County should want to start off in their new district with the good will of these new sister counties. Can this be accomplished if Sumter tries to snatch Mr. Moore's hard won seat in a race of only a week? This short time cannot be called a real campaign. Sumter County should think of future good will in the new district, and not try to throw its weight just because it has the largest number of voters in the district.

Do not destroy the friendly feeling of our new senatorial counties. If you believe in fair play, give Mr. Homer Moore the courtesy of serving the term he has already won. He is A-1 in his home area. He will serve Sumter County well.

signed, SUMTER COUNTY
FRIENDS OF HOMER MOORE

In my first advertisements, not having a similar specific issue, I just emphasized my educational background, my community service, and the fact that we had fairly close relatives in several of the counties. Almost immediately, though, as I was confronted with the effectiveness of Homer's claims even in my own county, I answered them more forcefully.

My response, as published on October 13 in the *Times-Recorder*, was

A STATEMENT BY JIMMY CARTER

My opponent, to get your sympathy, is insinuating to the voters of the 14th Senatorial District that he has already been elected as your Senator and that it is unfair for anyone from Sumter County to run against him. This is not true. The facts are these:

1. The 14th District consists of 7 counties—Sumter, Webster, Terrell, Stewart, Chattahoochee, Quitman, and Randolph, with a combined population of 74,553. These counties were formerly in 4 different old Senatorial Districts.

2. My opponent ran ONLY in his home county to represent one of these old districts. There were 1,635 votes cast and he received 552 of these votes or less than 35% of the votes cast in his county.

3. My campaign did not come as a last minute surprise to him, as I announced a week before the qualifying date. In fact, I qualified with the State Democratic Executive Committee before my opponent did. He had every opportunity not to qualify if he objected to competition.

My only purpose in this statement is to answer the questions raised by the advertisements of my opponent. This is a hard race between him and me and I will certainly appreciate your vote and support.

(signed) JIMMY CARTER

Without stopping his basic advertisement, Homer came back on October 15, just before election day, with this one:

TO THE VOTERS
OF SUMTER COUNTY:

A statement has been made by my opposition that my supporters tell a falsehood when they say that I was elected from all three of the counties in the Old 12th District. I am sure there was no intention of this in the statement—my friends just give the people credit for knowing the rules of the old rotation system. For my opposition to bring this up is begging the question and insulting to the intelligence of the voters. I would have served the three counties equally under the rotation plan. Everyone knows this.

My opposition also questions the statement that my supporters make in saying that the Counties of Stewart, Webster, and Quitman are the only ones in the New 14th District not separated from old friends to create the New District, and that Sumter is a new sister in the above. These are true facts, and my opponent is badly informed if he states otherwise. Other Counties also were moved from old friends and added to the four just named. They are: Randolph and Terrell, and Chattahoochee. The public knows this because it keeps up with the news.

I paid my first fee for this race last April, and stated upon election that I was a candidate again when reapportionment rules were made. I am very grateful to the people of the 14th District for evidence of their support. I earnestly ask that you go to the polls and vote for Homer Moore for the Senate. I will serve you well, and I will serve the District equally.

To the extent that it can be defined, the basic issue between me and Homer Moore was whether the conservative political establishment would be preserved against a total newcomer to politics who was known to be at least moderate on the segregation question. In the extremely abbreviated campaign, we never had a chance to debate or to confront each other in a public forum of any kind. Homer had raised the question of sportsmanship and fairness, aligning himself against me and the external forces from Washington that had disrupted Georgia's historic political system and, indirectly, were trying to reverse decisions already made by voters in the district. My main opposition, even in Sumter County, came from public officials who had more confidence that Homer would be compatible with the existing political system and their philosophy on the major issues of the day. But I had been involved in a multitude of community projects and was known by public officials as an activist and relatively independent in making decisions. When I received the endorsement of the editors of the *Americus Times-Recorder*, the key sentence of their editorial read: "Jimmy Carter has shown his courage of conviction and stood for what he considered right, sometimes in the face of strong opposition among his own people, and still retained their respect and friendship. This is an important attribute for a man in public office, since win or lose, he must retain the respect and confidence of his colleagues and constituents." Although these differences between me and Homer were subtle, they would shape the outcome of the election.

As I drove around the district the last few hours before election day, I kept my car radio on, pushing the three buttons that shifted from the two stations in Americus to the one in Terrell County. Nothing much had changed from day to day, and there was little news reporting about our race. The best way to change our paid statements was to drive to each of the radio stations, revise a few words in the text to bring it up-to-date, and read the new version into a tape recorder.

I was nervous all day on election eve, because I had said that I would make a brief television announcement that evening. To be on camera would be a new experience for me, and I struggled to memorize my statement as I drove around the district. I wanted to make a videotape recording so that it could be edited or done over if I froze, forgot my lines, or made a serious mistake, but the producers at the Columbus CBS station required me to give my three-minute speech live. The statement was a combination of my original biographical announcement and a brief answer to Homer's claim that he was already the elected senator. Rosalynn and my mother said I "did good" but looked nervous.

Even though I could not be sure who would receive more votes the next day, I was proud just to be a part of what everyone knew was a new political era. I mostly considered the hourly developments in the race itself and thought about what a victory might bring to me and my family, and how our lives might be changed.

chapter 4

✫✫✫✫✫✫✫✫✫✫✫✫✫✫✫✫✫✫✫✫✫✫✫✫✫✫

Confrontation
at Georgetown

I got up early on election day, October 16, went downtown to vote, and began driving to the seven courthouses
and some of the key voting precincts in the district. Rosalynn would have to operate the warehouse by herself, while
continuing her phone calling to encourage our known supporters to go to the polls. We agreed that I would call in
every hour or so to take any messages and to give her a
report on what was happening. I knew a number of the
officials at the polling places, and all of us felt free to exchange pleasantries so long as I didn't attempt to do any
politicking among the people waiting to vote. I was able to
make a fairly good judgment of the political atmosphere
just from the degree of warmth with which the election
officials in the different counties treated me.

My first stop was in Americus, about nine miles east of Plains. There was a short line at the courthouse, and I was told that so far the turnout was smaller than usual. This was troublesome here in my home county, but I reassured myself that it was still quite early and, after all, the race had received as much publicity here as in any other county. A uniformly low turnout, I reasoned, should have an equal effect on me and Homer Moore. Most of those who were voting anywhere in the district had only had a chance to hear a few radio spots or perhaps read some of our newspaper ads. I drove from there to the small town of Andersonville, home of the famous camp for Yankee prisoners during the Civil War and the easternmost voting place in the district. Mayor Lewis Easterlin was running the election and came out to say, "Jimmy, your opponent never did come to Andersonville, and he won't get many votes around here." (I carried the precinct 31–4.)

It was a different story farther south, in Leslie. The poll officials were still angry about the school consolidation fight and were obviously unfriendly. (This was the only place I lost in my own county, by twenty-nine votes.) Then I came back to Sumter City, where Rosalynn's great-uncle John Wise was the precinct chairman. "You've only lost two votes so far," he said. I asked him how he could be sure, and he said the people there were his neighbors, most of them kinfolks, and they were not reluctant to express their preference. (The vote turned out to be 38–2.) After these few visits, I was reasonably pleased with the way things seemed to be going in Sumter County.

Since it was on my way to the next county, I drove back through Plains, where Rosalynn told me that she had gotten a telephone call early in the morning from her cousin

Ralph Balkcom in Quitman County. He thought I should know that some disturbing things were going on at the courthouse over in Georgetown—worse than he had ever seen before. Since this was on the far western border of the district, I wanted to visit some of the other counties first. I called our close friend in Americus John Pope, who had offered to help if necessary, and asked him to go see what Ralph had to report. I would join him in two or three hours. I also called the *Columbus Enquirer* newspaper office and asked them to send someone to Georgetown to witness and report on the alleged improprieties.

My next stop was Webster County, where the officials were obviously either embarrassed or unfriendly. This was a disappointment, but I realized that Homer Moore's wife was from there and that he knew and traded with a lot more people in the county than we did. I was encouraged when I got to Terrell County, where we had a lot of peanut and cotton customers. I encountered several members of a square dance group with whom we had met weekly at the local American Legion club over the last two years to practice our increasingly fancy steps. They had become personal friends and were helping us during the election.

In Randolph County, which was too far from Plains for me to have known anyone except in the Lions Clubs, I only visited the courthouse and two of the rural precincts that were near the main highway. Since I didn't know much about the county, I just exchanged a few remarks with the folks around the voting places, let them know I was interested in the election, and then drove northward to Georgetown.

Although I had been to Georgetown only a couple of

times during the previous week to seek support, I wasn't too concerned about what might happen there. This was the second-smallest county in Georgia, with a total population of 2,400, with less than half of the adults white and likely to vote. Its popular vote wouldn't make much difference in the election. Moreover, Quitman had been in Homer Moore's old three-county district, and I knew that Homer's campaign manager, Sam Singer, had served in the legislature for several years with Joe Hurst, who was well known to be the political boss in the county. Hurst had made it plain to me on my last visit to the county that he was supporting my opponent, but some of the other leaders in the county had made it equally clear that they were strongly against Hurst and anyone he might endorse. Sharply and rigidly divided, the voters were much more likely to make decisions based on their friendships and animosities than on anything either Homer or I could have done during the brief campaign.

★ ★ ★

Every statewide candidate and all his own neighbors knew that, one way or the other, Joe Hurst could control the outcome of an election in Quitman County if he wanted to exert his maximum influence. Originally an outsider, he had risen to political power slowly but steadily, on the strength of his shrewdness and single-minded determination. When he had first moved over from Alabama as a young man in the late 1920s, he ran a small service station and beer joint on the Randolph-Quitman county line, called the Last Chance. Quitman was a "wet" county, allowing beer sales, while Randolph was totally "dry." This was the last chance for motorists leaving Quitman County to buy a beer or other refreshments of a stronger nature sold from under the counter. Later, Joe opened a place called the Monte Carlo, between Georgetown and the Chattahoochee River, where customers could find hard liquor and slot machines. He got in trouble with the law from time to time, but that didn't stop his providing the services desired by many of his neighbors. Although convicted a few times, he was never punished. There was a real advantage in mixing business and politics.

Joe ran for county commissioner every chance he got and was finally elected in 1935. He got a bigger break in 1942, when he led Ellis Arnall's successful gubernatorial campaign in Quitman County. Arnall was one of Georgia's more progressive governors and also a shrewd politician. He had a lot to gain from an alliance with Joe Hurst, and Joe began what was to be a steady career on the state payroll, first in the Highway Department, then in the Revenue Department, and finally with a better job for the commissioner of agriculture.

In 1949 Joe was elected to the state House of Representatives in a special election, and he continued to capitalize on his ability to deliver the two unit votes from his county. Small as it was, Quitman had one-third as many unit votes as all of Atlanta. Joe had a good feel for politics and was most often able to pick the prospective victor. He concentrated his efforts on elections for influential offices, like governor, lieutenant governor, and commissioners of agriculture, labor, and revenue. Of special concern to him were state judges and prosecuting attorneys. In these elections, Quitman County voters would rarely have an intense interest in the outcome. Whenever he supported such a winning candidate, Joe was able to parlay the victory into attractive benefits, both for his county and for himself. The six-lane expressway going through Georgetown (whose population in the 1990 census was still only 913) remains as testimony to his influence in Atlanta.

In local races, political and family interrelationships were more likely to be intense and issues more personal. In such cases, it was counterproductive to try to control the outcome unless the office was of vital concern to him. Joe would naturally be deeply involved in deciding who would be the sheriff or voter registrar, and he was careful to control the county Democratic executive committee, of which he served as chairman. However, he often stayed aloof from contests such as those for school superintendent or even county commissioner, where the outcome was not of special concern to him. When he used his influence in these secondary elections, it was to pay old political debts or to build alliances for the future.

As the years passed, and an increasing number of state officials came to owe their success in part to him, Joe Hurst was regarded as one of the more powerful men in Atlanta. Even when he happened to guess wrong in a governor's election, he was quick to repair the political damage. In 1958, for example, Quitman's two unit votes went to a right-wing candidate named William Bodenhamer, while Ernest Vandiver won the most overwhelming primary victory in the history of the state. When the legislature convened the next January, Joe immediately set about mending fences: he introduced a resolution to name the proposed new bridge connecting Georgetown to Eufaula, Alabama, the Ernest Vandiver Causeway. Never before had the state named a public structure after an active politician, let alone one who had just been elected to office. One of Joe's fellow representatives stood up, saying, "Mr. Speaker, is the effect of this resolution to move the Quitman County vote from Bodenhamer to Governor Vandiver?" The Speaker replied, "The gentleman is correct." The bill passed.

Joe's political power and shrewdness brought him many rewards, and he was able to funnel state money to Quitman County in the form of jobs, roads, and business deals. Ralph Balkcom described how Hurst used his influence: "One time I went to Atlanta with Joe and followed him around. He went to all the departments, met the top people, and shook hands with them. The elected ones knew he could deliver the county and was in the legislature. They were very nice to him and would listen about jobs, roads to be paved, or other business that Joe covered that people in the county had asked him about. They were eager to please him. It was something to see."

Joe also knew how to make sound investments by narrowly focusing his influence when the time came to vote. Governor Vandiver, grateful for the causeway naming and needing legislative support for the bills he wanted passed, helped Hurst solidify his power base in the House of Representatives. The governor had promised to reform state government, and a special bill was passed forbidding all full-time state employees from serving in the legislature. However, there was an exception for those who had already worked for a certain number of years. Joe Hurst, not coincidentally, was the only member who had served that exact amount of time on the state payroll. This provision not only solidified his power but also eliminated some of the competitors who had been enjoying similar influence. Equally important was the political support that Joe gave the state superior court judge and the solicitor general (district attorney) who had jurisdiction over the grand juries and all criminal trials in Quitman County—making it all but impossible to get an impartial trial if Joe Hurst's interests were at issue.

Using his connections in Atlanta, Joe was able to consolidate even further his power at home through domination of the welfare system. About half the people in Quitman County were receiving some form of public assistance, and all the money came through the good offices of Representative Hurst and the local welfare director—who happened to be Mary Hurst, Joe's wife. Quitman was perhaps the only county in America in which welfare checks were not sent directly to the recipients; they were all mailed to the Hursts' post office box. Joe Hurst made a point of delivering many of these checks personally, a practice that would leave no doubt in people's minds to whom they owed their gratitude and how they ought to express it on election day. With some degree of latitude, county welfare officials could decide whose names were on or off the relief rolls.

Joe also controlled a good deal of unofficial power in Atlanta by running the poker game in the Henry Grady Hotel, which lasted through each legislative season. More of the state's business was probably conducted in the Henry Grady than in the state capitol, and a lot of deals were made around the card table. Former governor Gene Talmadge's driver had run the game since the early 1930s, but when the family's hold on state government declined with Herman Talmadge's move to Washington as U.S. senator, Joe recognized an opportunity. He made good use of his strong support for the new governor, Marvin Griffin, and by the end of Griffin's first year in office, in 1955, Hurst was running the game and reaping the benefits.

One of the regular poker players was Sam Singer, a state representative from Stewart County who came to admire Hurst's political savvy and skill. Despite the fact that Stewart County had more than three times as many people as Quitman, Sam recalled that "using all my influence in the legislature I was able to get five people in my county on the state payroll, while Joe had a lot more than twenty-five —he never would say how many. He knew how to get things for Quitman County, and maybe at times for his own benefit." After the Chattahoochee River was dammed in 1961, Sam bought some land along the new lakeshore but couldn't make any progress with its development until he brought Hurst in as a partner. Within two years the roads on the property were paved and running water was piped in, all at no expense to the two entrepreneurs.

It was through Sam that Joe Hurst met Homer Moore, who often went to Atlanta with Sam to socialize with the statehouse crowd in the Henry Grady Hotel and to participate in the poker games. Sam and Homer had been business partners, political allies, and personal friends, so when Homer decided to run for the state Senate early in 1962, Sam supported him against three opponents in Stewart County.

When I first announced my candidacy in early October, Ralph Balkcom tried to convince Joe Hurst that I was a strong candidate, but to no avail. Joe made a trip over to Americus, where he talked to people who either did not think I had a chance to win or disapproved of my stand on school consolidation or the race issue. He then came to Plains to call on his fellow representative Thad Jones, who had succeeded my father in the state legislature and whose wife, Irene, was a cousin of Rosalynn's. Thad, who by then had become one of Georgia's most zealous segregationists, told Joe that it would be a serious mistake to give me any support and that I would not even carry my hometown. This was all Joe needed to convince him that Homer Moore would be the winner and was worthy of his endorsement. After he announced his choice, it became a matter of personal honor and political prestige to assure that his candidate would win in Quitman County. At the time, I knew practically nothing about this background.

The election in Quitman County shaped up as follows: Homer Moore had the support of Joe Hurst and the beneficiaries of his patronage—including those who held state jobs or received welfare payments. My supporters were some of the county commissioners, School Superintendent Ralph Balkcom, and a few other anti-Hurst people, including the Gary family, who generally lined up against Joe. The Garys had once been a dominant force in Quitman County politics, but since the 1940s Joe had aggressively gained power at their expense, especially after the death of the head of the family, State Representative (and occasionally Senator) Loren Gary, in 1949. I was not hopeful about a victory in Quitman County, but it seemed to me that there was enough anti-Hurst sentiment in the county to make the contest something of a horse race.

⋆ ⋆ ⋆

As October 16 approached, Joe Hurst was making his own preparations—but not of the sort one might expect. Sam Singer received a telephone call from Joe a day or two before the election, and this is how the conversation went:

JOE: How we doing?

SAM: Well, we're going to win. All our people are out working in the counties, we have a good organization, and folks know that Homer has already won once and in fairness ought to have the Senate seat. Things look real good.

JOE: Sam, I'm getting ready to stuff the ballot box.

SAM: Joe, there's no need to stuff it.

JOE: Well, I'm going to do it anyway.

SAM: Why, when it's not necessary?

JOE: Well, we do it every time, and I don't want my people to get out of practice.

"That's exactly what he told me," Sam recalled years later. "It made a big impression, and I'll never forget it. It was what they did in Quitman County, whoever was in power. It was done even before Joe Hurst got there."

Joe began his work on election day by altering the standard procedure for conducting elections in Quitman County. As chairman of the county Democratic committee, he directed his friend Sheriff Russell "Bub" Ogletree to move the voting place from the customary main courtroom to the office of the county ordinary, a local probate judge who settled minor disputes and was responsible for the proper conduct of general elections. The sheriff was happy to comply with Hurst's decision, since he had been elected with Joe's support and his brother Jim was the county registrar and the recipient of a job checking truck weights for the State Highway Department. He didn't even bother to consult with Robert Ellis, the man whose office they would be occupying.

When Ellis reported for work at his regular time, he was stunned to see what was transpiring. "It was an unusual thing to happen to a public official," he later recalled, "to come in your little office and find an election going on." Indeed, the available space in the ordinary's office was tiny, no more than four feet wide and with only five feet between the counter and the door. Joe Hurst and his confederates had chosen the space for that very reason, making it impossible for voters to have any privacy and very difficult for other observers to be present. In the main courtroom, where elections had always been held, the voting was simultaneously more public and more private: not only could people walk in and out and observe the proceedings but they could also go off by themselves to vote secretly after receiving their ballots from the officials. The voting booths, normally used even in Georgetown, were still folded and lying in the corner of the courtroom. In the ordinary's office, Ellis reported, it was as if "you came into the voting booth and there they were and they didn't leave and watched you vote." This was the scene that Ralph Balkcom had encountered when he showed up to vote, prompting him to call Rosalynn.

Ellis was unsure what, if anything, he should do. Running the election officials out of his office was a possibility, but Ellis was leery of defying Joe Hurst and didn't want to disrupt the election process, which was already under way. He expressed his displeasure, cast his own vote, and then decided to leave the courthouse for the day so as not to take part in what was happening. On his way out he ran into our friend John Pope, who had just arrived in Georgetown to follow up on Ralph's report of election irregularities. Ellis told John, "I know something is going to go on during the election, and I don't want to be any part of it. I came here to vote, and now I am going fishing and will not be back all day. I will take no part in the election and don't want to be accused of it!"

Inside, John saw immediately that Joe Hurst and his people were making a mockery of the voting process. He was barely able to squeeze in behind the door but managed to stay there through much of the day and watched the proceedings. There wasn't sufficient room for Ralph to stay with John, so he went out to the street and tried to encourage potential voters who might support me to go to the polls.

When he succeeded, those who entered the courthouse found they were not treading on neutral ground. According to John Pope's affidavit in court, Joe Hurst would typically meet voters at the door, greet them cordially, and then escort them into the ordinary's office, sticking close by while they cast their ballots. Doc Hammond, the assistant poll manager and one of Joe's closest associates, would lay the ballot on the counter along with a Homer Moore campaign card, saying, "Just scratch out Jimmy Carter's name. Joe wants you to vote for Homer Moore. Homer has already won this election twice and deserves to win today." If the voter showed any hesitation about following these instructions, the two men would use every means of persuasion to encourage a vote for Homer. Each ballot was then put into a cardboard box on the counter, through a large hole cut in the top.

Sometimes this persuasion got out of hand. John reported that on one occasion a woman named Rosalyn Moore (no relation to Homer) arrived at the courthouse to vote, only to be subjected to intense pressure from Doc Hammond. She hesitated, saying, "I don't know. I intended to vote for Jimmy Carter!" Doc then "became very verbal, letting her know that Joe wanted Homer to win" (in John's diplomatic phrase), and John stepped in, telling him, "Let her make up her own mind and don't harass her." Doc did not take kindly to this interruption—John later reported that he "cursed me out real good"—and continued badgering the woman until she finally scratched out my name from the ballot.

Hurst and Hammond, it seemed, would go to any lengths necessary to secure votes for Homer, even crossing the line into outright fraud. John observed what happened when an elderly couple, Mr. and Mrs. Spear, came to vote, and described the scene:

"They were met at the front door by Joe, who escorted them to the ordinary's office. Doc issued ballots to them and instructed them how to vote. Instead of voting there on the counter, they walked to the other end of the hall, placed their ballots up against the wall, voted, then folded their ballots several times, finally forming a very small knot of the paper, apparently in an attempt to keep Joe and Doc from seeing how they had voted. The Spears ran their hands through the five-inch hole in the cardboard ballot box to attempt to hide their personal ballots among the others.

"As they were walking away, Joe yelled out, 'Wait a minute, Mr. Spear, and let me see if you all have learned the right way to vote. You know I have been trying to teach you for a long time.' Joe then ran his hand into the ballot box, easily locating the two Spear ballots because of the way they were folded. He withdrew the slips of paper, looked at them and said, 'You haven't learned anything about voting my way.'

"Joe then tore up the two ballots and said, 'Give me some fresh ballots and let me teach them one more time.' Doc tore off six ballots and handed them to Joe. Joe openly scratched out Jimmy Carter's name on all six, folded them one time, placed them in the ballot box, all still together, and said, 'That's the way you are supposed to vote. If I ever catch you all voting wrong again, your house might burn down!' "

On recounting the testimony about what happened, I don't know if it is more surprising that Joe Hurst would engage in such blatant tactics or that he would do so in the presence of a representative of my campaign. He had been orchestrating election results for years and had always weathered challenges to his power. Apparently omnipotent within Quitman County, he felt that he could ignore the election laws with impunity before his seemingly helpless adversaries.

As the Spear incident shows, Joe Hurst and his people were not content with merely pressuring my supporters to change their votes: they also cast ballots for people who did not show up at the polls. Before my arrival in Georgetown,

Ralph and John decided to make a tour of the rural precincts in Quitman County, most of which were no less
under Joe's control. At their first stop, the poll manager
informed them that only about fifteen people had yet voted,
but John noticed that sixty-five ballots had already been
removed from a pad of one hundred. At the second polling
place, there was another suspicious count: the manager
there said only twenty or so people had voted, but the pad
of ballots showed that the precinct was up to number 72.
Fifty ballots missing from each of two precincts gave John
and Ralph good reason for concern, compounded by the
fact that the ballot box at the second stop was a shoe box
whose lid was not even taped shut and was presumably
removed to insert each ballot as it was cast.

Back in Georgetown, John confronted Joe with his
findings and told him that he was planning to report these
frauds and irregularities. Joe was not alarmed, replying, "I
have been running my county for twenty-seven years, my
way, and no one from Sumter County or any other county
is going to come in here and tell me how to do things. And,
Mr. Pope, I want you to know that I have put three men
in that river out back for doing less than you are doing
today."

✳ ✳ ✳

When I reached Georgetown around ten o'clock in the
morning, I drove directly to the courthouse, where I found
John and Ralph waiting for me. They began to describe
what was going on, with John doing most of the talking.
He was very excited, never having known of anything like
this before. Ralph, in contrast, was quite calm, interjecting

at times that, except for the voting place having been moved and no voting booths being used, this was not very surprising to him. He commented that he never bothered to vote anymore except in local races. People watched the proceedings much more closely then, and manipulation of the elections was less likely. But in contests that did not directly involve friends and neighbors, citizens had found the election would turn out the way Joe Hurst wanted, regardless of how the people voted. The abuses that day, however, were the most blatant that he had ever witnessed.

I called Rosalynn to give her a brief report on what I had been told, adding the reservation that John was excited and was probably exaggerating to some extent, and said that I would be staying in Quitman County longer than I had planned. Then I went just inside the entrance to the ordinary's office, where I stood quietly to observe as a couple of men voted.

The scene was just as John had described. Instead of voting booths there was a cardboard whiskey box sitting on an open counter. An irregular hole, about five inches in diameter, had been cut in the top of the carton. Adjacent to the box was a clear area about a yard wide, where the ballots were delivered to the voters and where they were expected to mark their choice. One of Homer Moore's campaign sheets was on the counter, adjacent to the ballot being marked. Joe Hurst and Doc Hammond were standing on either side of the voting place, ostentatiously watching as each person indicated a choice, folded the ballot, and dropped it in the hole. With one voter, Doc pointed to Homer's brochure and said, "This is the one Joe wants."

It was an amazing scene, permanently etched in my

memory. Hammond was in work clothes, which most people in town would be wearing. Hurst had on a white shirt and a gray fedora, pulled down low over his eyes. He was heavyset, had a swarthy complexion, and was smoking a cigar, and I could see how he could intimidate people. They both had glanced up to see me but didn't seem at all disturbed by my presence. Doc's attitude was obviously derived from Joe's reaction. When the voters had cast their ballots and left the room, I walked forward and asked, "Where are the voting booths?"

Joe said, "This is such a simple election, for just one office, that we've decided they're not necessary today."

"The law requires that people vote in secret," I replied, "and you're watching every one."

"The people don't mind if we know what they do."

"You're also trying to tell them how to vote."

Joe was quite at ease, seeming even to enjoy the exchange. He said, "They have a mind of their own. Nobody could make them do anything they don't want to do."

I said, "You are breaking a lot of laws. Who's in charge of the election?"

He replied, "Well, Doc here is the poll manager and I'm chairman of the Democratic committee, so I guess you might say we're in charge."

I then turned to Doc Hammond. "If you're the poll manager, you must know that the people have a right to vote without any interference from you."

Doc glanced at Joe and said, "I voted for Homer Moore and promised to politick for him, and I have a right to talk to people as I please."

I walked back to where I had been standing and spent

the next half hour or so either there or in the hall where I could view the voting place. On one occasion, I saw Joe take some ballots out of the box and examine them. During this period, Ralph brought in Robert McKenzie, who was then serving as state senator from the district. He joined me for a while to watch the voting. While he was there, Joe walked a few steps away, down the hall, leaving Doc to hand out the ballots and watch them being marked. There was no overt intimidation during that period, but the voters knew that Hurst would soon know how they had voted.

Senator McKenzie, John, Ralph, and I then walked out of the courthouse and assessed the situation. After a long discussion, we decided that Ralph and I would visit some of the rural precincts while John stayed at the court-house and made notes of what he observed. We found the voting still light and confirmed that there were some ballots missing. My hope was that if the Columbus news reporter I had called for would come and see what was going on, Joe might be forced to erect the voting booths and stop watching each voter's choice. That was not to be. When we drove up in front of the courthouse, I saw Hurst and a man sitting on the steps drinking Coca-Colas, obviously old acquaintances enjoying their discussion. When I walked up to them, Joe's companion didn't stand up but just said, "I'm Luke Teasley, with the Columbus paper."

I began to tell him what was happening, but he didn't seem very impressed. After listening for a while, Joe got up and walked inside. Teasley then took the initiative and said, "Mr. Carter, everybody knows it's not right, but this is the way they always run elections over here. I'm sure that the people who are for you will have their votes counted."

Now I got angry and demanded that he call in to Columbus and let his editor know what was happening in Georgetown. Teasley assured me that it wouldn't make any news. I asked him to go in the courthouse and spend a while just watching the procedure, but he said that he had to get back to the newspaper. He then got in his car and drove away.

I was, of course, worried about what was going on in Georgetown, but there was really nothing else that could be done except for John to stay and keep a careful record of what happened and to marshal as many other witnesses as possible among those Quitman County citizens who were not politically aligned with Joe Hurst.

I left to continue my visits to other counties and their voting places.

★ ★ ★

The afternoon proceeded much as the morning had, with John observing more proofs of fraud. At one point late in the day, the poll workers decided to take a refreshment break, with only one person, Bertha Barbaree, staying behind to watch the ballot box. John was out in front of the courthouse when he saw the other election officials leave, and he decided to go back to the ordinary's office to see what was happening. Entering the room quietly, he saw Mrs. Barbaree busily copying names directly from the registration list onto the numbered sheet of actual voters. "I watched this for about three minutes before making myself known," John recalled. "She was shocked at being caught and turned her pencil around and began madly erasing the last name she had just copied. She said, after some time, 'I made a mistake, and am trying to correct it.' "

It turned out that Mrs. Barbaree was not the only one putting extra names on the voter list to cover up Joe Hurst's stuffing the ballot box. Years later, Doc Hammond admitted that Hurst himself was guilty of the tactic: "He'd just take the list of voters, look down it, and say, 'This here one hadn't voted yet,' and he'd vote 'em. He'd come to the A's and then go on down, and vote 'em, like a damned fool."

Another irregularity took place at 6:45 P.M., about fifteen minutes before the polls were to close. One of the poll workers, Julia Pace, told John that it would probably take her and her colleagues all night to count the ballots— a statement that struck him as puzzling, since the voter list indicated that only 327 ballots had so far been cast. It should not take very long, he thought, for them to count so few votes. When he brought this fact to Mrs. Pace's attention, she replied, "But there are one hundred absentee ballots in the box to be counted."

"That's unusual," said John, "that so many could vote absentee in just a few days, and there being exactly one hundred. Are you sure of the number?"

"Yes," she answered. "Exactly one hundred." Recalling what he and Ralph had seen at the rural polling places that morning, John had a good idea of the source of those one hundred ballots. His suspicions were confirmed when he encountered Joe Hurst in the hallway about five minutes later and asked him how many absentee ballots he had received.

Joe's answer: "Not a one. I forgot to send the damn things out."

John had spoken to the Gary brothers earlier in the day about what Hurst was doing and asked them to stand by in case they were needed. As it turned out, one of the brothers, Tommy Gary, was on hand to observe the irregularities for himself. Tommy was a federal peanut inspector (and thus did not owe his livelihood to Joe Hurst) and by his own estimation was probably the only person in Quitman County who personally knew Homer Moore, Sam Singer, and me. We all owned warehouses and bought peanuts from farmers during harvest season. Tommy was responsible for observing our buying practices, and he had had good experiences with all of us. However, the Gary family had lined up behind my candidacy because Joe Hurst, their political enemy, was with Sam and Homer.

Tommy had been on the road during the day and arrived in Georgetown shortly before seven o'clock. He was surprised to find the election being conducted in the ordinary's office and decided to see what was happening in the few minutes before the polls closed. Tommy noted that his ballot was number 330 and that only three people came in after him. Just as the polls were closing, John saw Joe hiding some stubs, unused ballots, and the voter list in a paper sack, which he placed behind a set of law books on the ordinary's bookcase. John concurred with Tommy's count, having observed only six voters at the ordinary's office after his conversation with Julia Pace at 6:45.

The vote tally, however, told a different story. Although only 333 people had come to vote that day at the Georgetown courthouse, somehow the officials took 420 ballots from the box and counted them. The several witnesses in the room observed that some of the ballots were folded together, in packets of six or eight. When unfolded, these votes were unanimously for Homer Moore. Furthermore, it was determined later, only 410 names were re-corded on the registration lists, probably because John had interrupted Mrs. Barbaree before she was able to copy down the other ten names.

When the vote tally was announced, John, Ralph, and Tommy demanded to examine the ballots and confronted Joe Hurst with their own count of 333 as the total number of voters for the day. At that time, no one bothered to compare the number of ballots with the voter list to see if they matched. When asked to account for the discrepancies, Joe replied that Robert Ellis, the ordinary, had opened the polls early that morning and had overseen the casting of one hundred ballots, had locked up the stubs in his safe, and then had turned the polls over to Hurst and his people, who started with a new pad of five hundred ballots. John observed that this was a highly irregular procedure and demanded that Ellis be brought in to explain. Remembering his conversation with the ordinary earlier that day, John hoped to expose to the assembled observers the fraud that had taken place.

He asked one of the younger Gary brothers, who had just arrived at the courthouse, to fetch Robert Ellis, but Joe said that he would send one of his people to get him. Ellis arrived in a huff, shouting, "Where is that John Pope who is accusing me of stuffing the ballot box?"

John turned to face him and was met by a stinging attack: "Why are you accusing me of stuffing the ballot box? I purposely explained to you this morning that I was having nothing to do with this election, and now you are accusing me of fraud!"

John asked Ellis to think about the situation. "Do you

really think I said that, or do you think Joe Hurst told his man to tell you I said that?"

Ellis, a little shamefaced, apologized for his outburst and joined the others in examining the ballot box and questioning Hurst. Joe, however, had had enough. He picked up the box and shouted angrily, "The polls are closed! Let's all go home!"

John hurried to the front window and called for help. A group of men, assembled on the courthouse steps by the Garys, rushed into the building. They tried to get an explanation from Joe, asking, "Will you now tell us how you wound up with close to one hundred extra ballots in the box?"

Joe repeated his nonanswer. "Damn it," he bellowed, "I said the polls are closed. All of you get the hell out of here!"

Tommy Gary said, "No, Joe, we have gone along with you too long. You'll have to explain this."

John added, "Maybe I can help, Joe," as he walked across the room to the bookcase, from which he extracted the paper sack containing the voter list and ballot stubs. Laying them on the desk, he said, "Joe seems to have lost this."

Hurst then left the room, and in his absence John asked the remaining poll workers if they would admit before their fellow townspeople that there were about one hundred ballots in the box for which they could not account. They all admitted that to be the case.

Joe then returned to the ordinary's office with Solicitor General Joe Ray, and they took away the ballot box, which would be entrusted to Doc Hammond for safekeeping that night. Doc also took the stubs and the voter list, which he claimed Ellis gave him, and stuffed them in his shirt. While he would claim that he did not tamper with the ballot box that night, he was not so scrupulous about the list of voters. He admitted later that another Hurst associate had met him on the street as he left the court-house. Doc instructed him to "take this list on over to your house and get rid of it." It was dutifully burned.

The final unusual incident of this Quitman County adventure occurred as John Pope drove home that night. On his way out of Georgetown, a speeding car cut in front of him and ran him off the road. "I said to myself, 'This is it!' " John recalled. "I really thought that Joe had sent his men for me." The driver of the car was Loren Whitaker, one of Hurst's longtime supporters, who was on his own errand. He explained to John that he wanted to protect his daughter, Mrs. Elton Friedman, who had been working at the polls that day. He knew that she had listed many names on the voting register who were not legal voters, but she had done so on Hurst's orders. John promised Loren that he would try to keep his daughter out of the public eye if he would promise to help us gather evidence against Joe. Whitaker agreed, and John got back in his car for the long drive to Sumter County.

✯ ✯ ✯

While all these events had been going on in George-town, I had been experiencing the anticlimax and uncom-fortable anxieties of election day. Except for getting people to make telephone calls and arranging free rides to the polls for supporters who needed transportation, there was not much my family and I could do on that October Tuesday. Driving around and visiting polling places served primarily to keep me occupied. So far as I could tell, voting was proceeding normally in all the other counties.

Late in the afternoon I drove back to our warehouse, where Rosalynn and a few friends had gathered. We did some calculating of what kind of showing I would need to win the election. It would depend on a high turnout in our own county and just a reasonable vote in the counties where Homer had such a great head start.

Our first information on the vote came from Sumter County, where we had representatives at each voting place. We became increasingly concerned as we received the returns. I carried every voting district except Leslie and won the entire county by a three-to-one margin, but it seemed that only about one-third of the registered voters had gone to the polls. As we began to hear from other counties, we could see that the results would be very close. Neighboring Webster County turned out a big vote, and my support there was disappointing, but I was holding a lead of seventy-five votes in the whole district, not counting the Quitman County returns. We feared the worst, and John Pope's phone call that night from Georgetown confirmed our fears. Recounting the irregularities, he gave us the bad news: Homer Moore had carried the Georgetown precinct by 317 to 103 and the entire county 360 to 136.

One of the people at the warehouse with us that election night was Warren Fortson, an attorney from Americus whose older brother Ben was Georgia's secretary of state. Warren also recalled how we got sicker and sicker as we received the final returns from Quitman County. My mother, sitting on the floor of the warehouse, probably knew a lot more about politics than any of us there, and she said several times to Warren, "Jimmy's so naive, he's so naive."

I guess I was naive, as Mama said, and at that time extremely disillusioned with politics and the news media. With the recent court rulings and legislation in Atlanta to strike down the old county unit system and reapportion the legislature, my family and I had anticipated a new era in Georgia politics that would bring fairness, honesty, and maybe an end to racial discrimination. Now, we had witnessed a case of dishonesty and election fraud worse than we had ever imagined, and apparently nothing could be done about it. Not only would the newspapers not report the fraud but some of them seemed to be in league with the bosses themselves, if the *Columbus Enquirer* reporter was any representative. I could still see the grin on Joe Hurst's face, and the image burned me up. I had been betrayed by a political system in which I had had confidence, and I was mad as hell!

A small group of us discussed the situation for a couple of hours, with the prevailing sentiment being that it was a hopeless case. It was highly likely that I would just be considered a poor loser—an innocent who didn't understand the rough-and-tumble of south Georgia politics. We turned to Warren Fortson that night more than to anyone else, because he was the only lawyer there. He was cautious like the rest, reminding us that he had played a small role in an election contest involving a local judge's race a couple of years earlier. "All they would do is recount the ballots," he said.

In the middle of this discussion, I answered questions from the newspapers in Americus and Columbus about whether I was conceding that Homer Moore had won the nomination. After letting them know quite briefly that there were some problems with the vote count in Quitman County, I just said that I would have to wait for the official returns the next day.

We knew that, in addition to the legal issue, there would be a lot of politics involved. Since Warren was a relative newcomer to the community and was widely known as a liberal on the race issue, he advised me to talk to some of the more conservative and influential lawyers in Americus before making a final decision about whether to contest the election. Maybe one of them would take my case, if I decided to proceed. Otherwise, I should do the gracious thing and concede defeat. After all, none of us believed that Homer Moore had been party to what had happened in Georgetown. I had run a good race and made a respectable showing under the circumstances. Maybe that was enough.

✶✶✶✶✶✶✶✶✶✶✶✶✶✶✶✶✶✶✶✶✶✶✶✶✶✶✶✶✶✶✶✶

The Dead
Voted
Alphabetically

The morning after the election, Rosalynn and I got up earlier than usual to decide what we should do. Although we were disappointed, we agreed, first of all, that our lives could be full and gratifying regardless of whether I ever served in the legislature. We also counted up the potential costs in time, money, and embarrassment if we embarked on what was likely to be a fruitless and quixotic legal effort to overturn the election results. I think the deciding factor for me, however, was my determination not to be cheated. By breakfast time, I had decided to contest the election.

Reading the morning newspapers, we realized that we had forgotten that the state Democratic convention was being held in Macon that very day. Not having any legal help at the time, I called John Pope and asked him to drive over with me so I could present my case to the assembled officials. Rosalynn would just have to manage Carter's Warehouse one more day, supervising the peanut buying and cotton ginning in my absence.

As in the national conventions, Georgia's successful primary candidates would be officially acclaimed as the party's nominees. Then Governor-nominee Carl Sanders and other major candidates would make their acceptance speeches, and an entirely new slate of Democratic party officials would be chosen to serve for the next four years. We wanted to let the top officers know about our claim of fraud in Quitman County and thus prevent the convention's certification of Homer Moore as the Senate nominee from our district.

We stopped first at the offices of the *American Times-Recorder* so that the afternoon edition of the paper could report my possible plans to contest the election. I discussed with the editor what had happened in Quitman County. He was interested in my story, and, although I wasn't ready to announce a final decision, at least the headline reporting the election results read "Carter Considers Contesting Race." In the *Columbus Ledger* and the two weekly newspapers in the district, there was less equivocation. "Moore Wins," "H. L. Moore Elected," and "Richland Businessman Nominated" were how they played the story.

John and I then drove the ninety miles over to Macon. When we found the civic center where the convention was being held, the streets around it were filled with automobiles and the sidewalks with people. The newspapers would later report that there were 7,000 people there. To us, the civic center was a forbidding place. I don't remember any other time I have felt more out of place or when my efforts were more fruitless. We didn't know anyone there and had no idea where to go. No one seemed to know who was responsible for anything. The Vandiver people were on the way out, and the Sanders replacements hadn't been officially confirmed in their offices. Somebody told us that a man named Charles Pannell had been mentioned as the likely chairman of a committee in charge of election contests, but we never found him.

Governor Ernest Vandiver was presiding and soon turned the gavel over to J. B. Fuqua, Sanders's choice for chairman of the state Democratic party. It seemed that almost all the delegates were Sanders people, there to cheer their champion and be recognized as members of the winning team.

Our efforts were a total failure. We were treated like lepers by some and by others as though we didn't exist. This was an exuberant crowd, primarily interested in being part of a celebration and looking out for their interests for the next four years. Those who were still in positions of authority were either being replaced that day or hopeful that they could inveigle appointments for themselves or their friends. They had absolutely no interest in an unknown newcomer to politics who was not willing to accept his own defeat with good grace. The ones who didn't ignore us were polite enough to shuffle us from one person to another until it was too late for anyone to consider our case. We eventually learned that the results of all the House and Senate races had been confirmed early that morning in a completely routine fashion, exactly as reported by the officials from the various districts. With these formalities out of the way, the afternoon was clear for the more important acceptance speeches.

We heard that there were fourteen contested elections in the state, and we eagerly searched for a list of them. All were districts in which no candidate had received a majority, and in each case a runoff election was to be held a week later between the two top men. We looked for a report on our district and found "14th District: Homer L. Moore, Richland." The election was over as far as the state party was concerned.

We came home disheartened but still angry and determined not to give up. What I needed most of all then was some legal advice. I knew and liked Warren Fortson, but, as he had suggested, I hoped to get one of the more prominent and influential lawyers in our county seat to take our case.

My first stop was to see Wingate Dykes, the Sumter County Democratic chairman, who was a longtime supporter of the Talmadges and the most politically influential lawyer in our county. He was also the brother-in-law of Superior Court Judge Tom Marshall, who had himself been the victorious candidate in a contested vote count two years earlier. Marshall and his opponent, Charlie Burgamy, had finished almost in a dead heat, but at the recount it was revealed that Burgamy had improperly solicited absentee ballots in about half a dozen cases—in some instances even signing the ballot as witness. These six invalidated votes were enough to turn the election decisively in Marshall's favor. If anyone would be sympathetic to a claim of electoral injustice, I thought, it would be a Marshall associate like Wingate Dykes. Furthermore, he had a long-standing connection to our family, having done most of the legal work for my father in the years before his death.

I had to wait awhile before getting in to see him. He listened to me closely and with apparent concern, and then replied, "Jimmy, this is a bad thing that happened, but there is no way any challenge can be successful. I helped Tom in his contest for judge, and I am thoroughly familiar with the law. All it permits is a recount. In a few counties, obviously including Quitman, they do things like you describe all the time and are experts at it. They know how to cover their tracks to avoid any challenges. Besides, the election was between two good men. We think a lot of Homer Moore, who gave Tom full support in his election over in Stewart County and was a key factor in his being judge now."

This was discouraging, but I couldn't really disagree with anything Wingate had said. I then went by to talk to Billy Smith, an equally prominent lawyer who had been one of the county leaders in supporting Carl Sanders for governor. This connection with the governor nominee could be quite helpful if we hoped to gain any support in Atlanta for our case. However, when I arrived, Billy was not in his office. It was getting late, so I decided to call on Warren. My plan was to let him know what Wingate had said and ask him to represent me.

Warren understood the nuances of my situation as well as the specific charges. He recognized that profound racial antagonisms lay beneath the surface of the bosses' strong-arm tactics. In many Georgia communities, like Quitman County, blacks were a majority of the population, and established power brokers like Joe Hurst perceived that the blacks could take over politically if they were to band together to vote. The convoluted and discriminatory election laws and customs thus served not only to make it hard for white leaders outside the system to challenge it but also to keep black people in their place.

Warren had also played a key role in Judge Marshall's disputed election in 1960, serving as Marshall's vote counter in the successful recount. In the process, as Wingate Dykes had said, they all learned a lot about Georgia's antiquated election code. There were few men more savvy than the veterans of the Marshall campaign. When I met with Warren, however, he warned me that the laws as written were not a powerful tool against election irregularities and that the only challenge that might be successful would be simply to ask for a recount of the ballots for accuracy.

Those caveats notwithstanding, Warren was as eager as I was to challenge the domination of Georgia politics by county bosses that, at least in this case, had survived the abolition of the county unit system. He could see that I had not been fully dissuaded by Wingate's arguments, so we decided that we would review the election laws and the official results from all counties in the district and then decide what to do about the election.

That night I called Ralph Balkcom to let him know about my tentative plans to contest the election, and that Warren and I would come to Georgetown to discuss the matter with him, Senator McKenzie, and the Gary family.

We drove over to Georgetown the next morning, which was two days after the election. It would be the first of many such trips, and we learned to recognize every turn in the road, the churches, settlements, barns, and crops along the way. Plains was where my Carter ancestors and Rosalynn's Smith and Murray families had lived for four or five generations; then, heading west, it was nine miles to Preston, with our family farm about halfway; then the same distance to Richland, where my mother was born and had lived with her father, Jim Jack Gordy, and his large family until she came over to our hospital in Plains to become a registered nurse and met my father; then it was nine more miles to Lumpkin, not far from the tiny country settlement of Brooklyn, where my grandfather had moved into Stewart County to teach school before my mother was born; then twenty-seven miles farther through relatively uninhabited rolling hills to Georgetown and the Chattahoochee River. It had always been strange to me that all the distances between towns were multiples of nine miles. We thought it might have something to do with the distance between desirable rest stops for the first travelers. In any case, with the exception of Quitman County, my family had deep roots in these communities, and Warren was to learn a lot about my family history on our trips together.

When we arrived in Georgetown, there was a small group of people, including Ralph Balkcom, in front of the courthouse. The Gary brothers immediately came to join us from their nearby store, and, after the word spread, twenty or thirty people assembled near the courthouse steps, creating something of a hubbub around us. They eagerly recounted stories of political shenanigans in the county, leaving no doubt that those who had anything to say were eager for me to contest the election and were ready to help in the effort.

With these assurances, I mounted the top step of the courthouse and announced that I had decided to file an official demand for a recount and would try to expose what had happened in the county. The crowd applauded, and I promised to be back the next day to bring the necessary documents.

On the trip home, Warren outlined to me what he remembered from the Georgia election code, and when we got to his office in Americus he gave me a small booklet entitled "Rules and Regulations of the State Democratic Executive Committee of Georgia," dated April 18, 1962. Since the contested election was a Democratic primary, this was the current and authoritative text. As mentioned earlier, for almost a century Georgia laws had been modified to conform to the policies of the Democratic party leaders, so the state laws and party rules were inextricably entwined.

There is still a rusty paper clip on page 24 of my copy, where, under section IX, the paragraph begins, "If there shall be a recount of the ballots in any county . . . ." It goes on to say that the results of a recount in a county shall be filed with the county executive committee and for statewide offices with the chairman of the state committee. These officials of the Democratic party would then certify the final results to the secretary of state, who would direct that the name of the nominee be entered on the general election ballot as the party choice for that office.

We knew that a recount like ours was to be supervised by a senior superior court judge from a judicial district adjacent to the one in which the election had been held, who would therefore be likely to perform this duty in an unbiased way. In our case, this would be the best route to avoid the domination of Joe Hurst and his county committee. However, a recount was considered to be a purely mathematical process, simply counting the votes again after individual challenged ballots had been closely examined to determine if they had been clearly marked. It was not exactly a recount that we were seeking but a challenge to the integrity of the entire process in Quitman County, or at least in Georgetown.

Article XII of the Democratic party rules covered this rare contingency: "Should any candidate desire to contest the result of the primary election in any county upon grounds not contemplated or provided for by said Act [covering recounts], he shall, within five days from the date of said primary, file with the Secretary of the County Executive Committee written notice of said contest, which shall set forth in detail the grounds thereof. In the absence of the Secretary, such notice may be filed with any member of the County Executive Committee."

This was a chilling prospect, knowing that our choice was between a simple recount in a fair forum or presenting our allegations of fraud to the very people who had perpetrated it—Chairman Joe Hurst and his Quitman County Democratic Executive Committee.

Another concern was the time involved for the entire process, which was especially tight given the last-minute nature of this special election. The contest had to be filed within five days, and the county committee was required to certify the results to the state executive committee within ten days, following which there was a five-day period for filing an appeal, again to the county committee. Following appellate court rules, only newly discovered evidence could be submitted for consideration at this point. Three more days were authorized for the appellate procedure and reporting the results to the state committee. We added up the days permitted for the entire process, most of which would depend on the schedule to be set by the Quitman County Democratic officials. It was now October 18, and the general election would be on November 6, just nineteen days away. We calculated that eighteen days were allowed after we filed our contest for the results to be submitted to the state committee.

After this, a lot would have to be done, all in the one remaining day before the election. When the state Democratic officials assessed the decision of the county committee, they would have to make a judgment, then certify the victorious candidate to the secretary of state, who would have the official nominee's name printed on the state ballots. These would then be distributed to county ordinaries, thence to the precinct chairmen, for use on general election day. It looked almost hopeless.

We decided that we had no choice but to make every effort to stay out of the clutches of Joe Hurst and the local committee he dominated. Although certainly not a promising route, we would file for a recount, knowing that the custom was for challenged individual ballots to be examined closely to determine the intent of the voters, to throw out those where the choice could not be determined, and then to count those that were left. It would be almost unprecedented to discard clearly marked ballots on the ground that the election procedures had been faulty. We also knew full well that Hurst and the other election officials had plenty of time to doctor the documents so that no fraudulent evidence would be found.

With the exception of the brief article in the *Americus*

Times-Recorder, there was still no mention of the election discrepancies in the regional or statewide news media. This silence disturbed us, for we realized early on that we had to generate newspaper coverage if our challenge was to succeed. It was only through publicity that we could get beyond the simple counting of ballots and increase the public awareness and political significance of Joe Hurst's fraudulent practices. We took the first crucial steps that Thursday night, October 18, when Rosalynn, Warren, John Pope, and I met at the home of my cousin Hugh Carter to explore our possibilities and try to dispel the apparent hopelessness of our case.

After a long, rambling discussion, Hugh finally said, "Why don't we call my brother Don? He was city editor of the *Atlanta Journal* for several years and might have some ideas about how to get someone in Atlanta to take an interest."

We got Don on the phone in Washington, where he was managing editor of the *National Observer*, a new nationwide newspaper that was being published by Dow Jones. I described what was going on and told him we needed some publicity.

He listened carefully, asked a few questions, and then said, "There is one of the most outstanding investigative reporters I know who still works for the *Journal*. His name is John Pennington, and he happens to be from Andersonville, in Sumter County. He's fearless and has never backed down from a tough assignment. I don't know what he might be doing right now, but I can find out and call you back."

Don was as good as his word. I talked to John Pennington that night, and he said almost immediately that he would fly to Americus in his small plane, get some more answers to questions that Don hadn't been able to answer, and decide what he ought to do.

When Pennington arrived the next morning, Warren and I let him examine all our files and explained our case in detail. Then he decided to go to Georgetown. I offered to give him a ride, but he refused, saying that he wanted to stay at arm's length from me from now on and try to report all sides of the controversial issues. He would just ask me questions, as he would Homer Moore, Joe Hurst, and others. He was willing, however, to let John Pope chauffeur him around when he came into the area through Americus. When he decided to fly in to Columbus, he would rent a car for himself. That's what he did most of the time. Because of his insistence on independence, Pennington never talked to me during the succeeding days except in a professional manner.

Since to a great degree my election challenge depended on this reporter, we tried to learn more about him. It turned out that John Pennington and I had a lot in common. He was born a month before I was, just a few miles from where we lived at the time. He grew up in a rural community, his father was a farmer, and he said one of the biggest events in his life was when the electric power lines reached his home. We had both attended Georgia Southwestern College in Americus, but after that our lives were quite different. He went on to study journalism at the University of Georgia and became editor of the student newspaper *Red and Black*, as my cousin Don Carter had done some years earlier. It was Don, as city editor of the *Atlanta*

Journal, who had given John his first job as a reporter. An even earlier family relationship was that John's father had often traded mules with my uncle Alton Carter, Don's father.

John Pennington was a crusader and quickly became a well-known investigative reporter. He submitted his articles for publication only after he had completed meticulous personal work at the places and among the people involved. He was intense about his work and about flying, which he took up a few years after going to work with the *Journal*. With his own small plane, he was often the first reporter from the major news media to arrive at the scene of a crime or disaster. In fact, on several occasions he flew to the coasts of Georgia and the Carolinas when an oncoming hurricane was expected to strike.

In the late 1950s he had written a series of thirty articles exposing gross abuses in the Georgia prison system, which almost certainly helped to inspire a successful prison reform program in the state. Particularly unforgettable was a photograph John had taken of an inscription on the wall of a cell that had been occupied by a man who had died in the electric chair. The crudely scrawled words were "They is no God."

John was an avowed enemy of the Ku Klux Klan. Once, at a Klan rally, he approached closely the hooded members and photographed them. They surrounded him, some with shotguns, and demanded that he give them his camera. He refused and stood there defiantly. "You'll have to kill me first," he said. After some discussion among the Grand Dragon and other leaders, they decided not to murder a news reporter. The Klansmen opened a pathway and let John walk away, still carrying his camera.

As John listened to our tale of electoral fraud in Quitman County, he grew increasingly sympathetic to our cause. Each allegation made him more eager to get to the bottom of the story and expose Joe Hurst and what his people had done. "I knew I had a story," he would later recall. "As a fellow native of their county, I shared the outrage. Jimmy Carter's state Senate victory had been blatantly stolen." Fired by indignation and a sure sense of a good story, John Pennington would not rest until the facts were laid bare for the people of Georgia to judge for themselves.

★ ★ ★

On Friday afternoon, October 19, we mailed our recount requests to the Democratic executive committees in six of the counties and drove back to Georgetown to deliver our documents in person. We wanted the clock to begin ticking as early as possible.

Even this official challenge did not create much of a stir in the district. On Saturday a small article on page 9 of the *Columbus Enquirer*, the main area newspaper, reported my allegations concerning the disparity between votes cast and ballots counted in Georgetown. This same information made the front page of the *Times-Recorder* in Americus, including a statement by County Chairman Wingate Dykes that the recount in Sumter County would be conducted on Monday, October 22.

During all these days I was swamped with work. I still had to tend to the warehouse business. We were recleaning, drying, grading, and unloading peanuts, ginning and buying cotton, and settling up the annual bills of our customers. Rosalynn was doing must of the book work, keeping the accounts current and figuring the farmers' debts to us against the value of the crops we had bought from them. She and some good helpers could also weigh the trucks and farm trailers and take care of the routine transactions. The few customers who would deal only with me and not my wife, a woman, would have to wait a little longer to get paid or to settle up accounts.

Also, the heart of our business was seed peanuts. This was extremely complicated, for almost a dozen varieties had to be kept separate as they came in from large and small fields on our own farms and those of a number of farmers with whom we had growing contracts. For each variety, following breeder seed from the experiment stations, there were three or four generations within which the lineage had to be kept pure and documented: foundation, registered, and then one or two years of certified seed. The first year there would be only a few hundred pounds of breeder seed issued by the agricultural scientists, but this quantity would expand rapidly as each seed peanut produced an average of about fifty more to be planted the following season. At that time, we were shelling the state's foundation seed in addition to our own. This was a great responsibility, and I was the only one who knew all the fields and could avoid having any of the hundreds of trucks and farm trailers unloaded in the wrong place.

Nevertheless, the election challenge had become an obsession with me, and our regular customers understood that I had to be gone from the warehouse for a few working hours each day. As best we could, Warren and I established a daily routine, meeting at the warehouse when it could be arranged, reviewing the latest developments, then driving over to Quitman County to get affidavits from everyone we could find who had any information to give us. We soon learned how deeply the county was split politically between those who were for Joe Hurst and those who were against him. It was an exhausting schedule. Warren and I got very little sleep, and we frequently forgot to eat as well.

Georgetown was a small community of homes and a few stores along State Route 27 as it descended from a hilly area toward the bank of the Chattahoochee River. The population of the county had dropped 20 percent during the previous decade, from 3,000 to about 2,400, and the vacant store buildings along the main street presented vivid testimony to the county's declining economy. The courthouse was the center of activity, but this was true only in relative terms. As John Pennington was to point out after spending several days there, "most of the time the courthouse is virtually deserted. . . . Most county officials do not keep their courthouse offices open. Instead, they leave a telephone number on the door where they can be reached if needed. Normally the only offices open on a daily basis are those of the health, welfare, and school departments."

Warren and I would return from Quitman County late in the day, perhaps eat a quick supper, and then usually work as late as we could stay awake with the evidence, affidavits, and a study of court cases that might be pertinent to our case. I became an eager legal assistant, laboriously examining old decisions, looking up cross-references, and writing out paragraphs that I thought might be pertinent. Warren was doing the same thing while trying to formulate a coherent legal strategy. We also spent long hours making copies (on old-fashioned Thermofax machines) of the statements we were accumulating and the official papers we decided to file with the courts and political committees.

Our biggest problem during those days was persuading Quitman County people to talk to us openly and forthrightly. We did not blame the reluctant ones, because those with the most valuable information were also most vulnerable to Joe Hurst's intimidation. These were welfare recipients, people working for the state, the naturally timid and weak, and all who could be hurt if their kinfolks lost their income. It was their general belief that nothing could possibly shake Hurst's control of the county. Even a loss in this particular race would not have any permanent effect on the local people. When Jimmy Carter was gone, senator or not, Joe Hurst would be there in Georgetown, still in charge. Yet people did come forward. Even today I find it amazing that so many were willing to endanger their financial and maybe physical well-being to bring free elections to their county and to escape from domination by such a powerful man.

That much said, the fact remained that many of the people of Quitman County did not consider Joe Hurst a villain. He was a powerful and influential man, yes, but in many cases he benefited from genuine friendships and from calling on the obligations of those who knew him as their benefactor. He was also known to be extremely accommodating to anyone who came to him for help with a problem, and he had done a lot for the community. At the same time, we quickly learned that many people in the county were afraid of Hurst's anger. We heard a lot of rumors about his past arrests for fairly serious crimes, but we discounted these stories as little more than political spitefulness. (It was revealed in a trial two years later that he had been indicted on at least eight previous occasions, including one arrest for assault with intent to murder, and had been found guilty in five of those cases. However, because of his influence with the local superior court judge and solicitor, his punishment had always been minimal or nonexistent. He had never paid a significant fine or served a day in jail.)

Warren went with me on most of the visits to Georgetown, but sometimes I went alone while he stayed in Americus to conduct our legal case. From our earliest trips until the process was over, a sedan would be parked and waiting for me as I crossed the line from Stewart into Quitman County. Then the car would follow me into Georgetown and park adjacent to mine. When I got out, so did the two men working for Hurst. Ostentatiously, they would follow me wherever I went. If I talked to Ralph Balkcom, one of the Garys, or other prominent political opponents of Joe Hurst, the men would stand a few steps away. If I approached any of the less influential people in the county, one of the men would stand within arm's length of me so he could obviously overhear every word. Sometimes both of them would do this. They were polite, rarely spoke to me or my companions, but were persistent. They never went into a private home with me, but on several occasions they followed me into someone's yard. If I drove over to Eufaula for lunch, they would wait on the Georgia side of the bridge until I returned, then follow as before until I left Quitman County in the afternoon, heading home.

I was not really afraid of them, but they made me uneasy. It was obvious that they were intimidating some of the people from whom we were seeking statements about such things as whether they actually voted, whom they saw in the courthouse when they were there, their relationship with Hurst, how they received their welfare checks, or whether they had been influenced in casting their vote.

Sometimes people would talk privately to Ralph, who would then relay their statements to us, but this was not what we needed. We had to use sworn affidavits to challenge individual votes for the recount and attempt to establish a pattern of intimidation or fraud that might discredit the entire election. Including those from some of the strongest anti-Hurst people, we accumulated thirty affidavits substantive enough to be submitted in court.

One night I came back from Georgetown and found Rosalynn in tears. She told me that a farmer who had never traded with us before had come to Carter's Warehouse with a truckload of peanuts to sell. This was a relatively rare event, except when the peanuts were damaged in some way and the owner drove around from one place to another hoping to get lucky with a better grade. In this case the peanuts were of high quality, having been grown in Stewart County, according to the farm marketing card. While his truck was being unloaded into our storage warehouse, the stranger sat around our office with some other farmers, who were drinking Cokes and eating the deep-fried, salted shelled nuts that we always provided for our customers.

After a few minutes he walked over to Rosalynn, who was at the calculator figuring the price per ton on his load of peanuts and waiting for the empty truck weight to determine how much to pay him. He said he had a message for her. Someone wanted us to know that the last time anyone had crossed Joe Hurst, their store burned down. Rosalynn was startled, of course, and asked him who sent the message, but the farmer replied that he had relayed all he was supposed to say. When he received the check for his peanuts he drove away, and we never heard from him again. I reassured Rosalynn as much as possible, but both of us were worried about the threat.

***

Within four days after the election, we had gotten affidavits that covered most of the points we wanted to make. Now, Warren and I decided that we should pursue both routes in our contest. In addition to our petition to recount votes, we would demand that the Quitman County Democratic Executive Committee throw out the entire Georgetown box because it was so shot through with fraud that there was no way to tell how the people had voted. We delivered this second petition on Saturday, October 20.

Warren and Homer Moore's attorney, Jesse Bowles, agreed that the recount proceedings in the other six counties would be postponed until the Quitman County protest could be heard. (Later, one of Homer's legal challenges would be based on the absence of a recount of all ballots in the district.) Following the standard procedure for the Quitman County dispute, a three-person recount committee was impaneled, consisting of one representative from each of the campaigns and the most senior superior court judge from an adjoining district to serve as the "umpire." We named Billy Horne, a friend from Americus, as our representative, while Homer picked Sam Singer. The senior judge turned out to be Carl Crow, from the town of Camilla in Mitchell County, about sixty miles south of Plains.

The delivery of legal papers between Homer's group

and mine became quite a game. Later in the case, when the lawyers had gotten well acquainted with each other, they didn't have much trouble exchanging the documents among themselves in a timely and proper manner. At first, though, we would have to hunt for members of the Quitman County Democratic committee, most often just finding them in their homes or where they worked. As in Plains, a community about the same size, one's whereabouts were usually known. When Joe Hurst was in Georgetown, he would accept the legal papers with what seemed to be genuine nonchalance, sure of the fruitlessness of our efforts and either disdainful or amused. Homer and I would often have to find each other personally, and this was more difficult. It was not my impression that we deliberately avoided accepting service of the notices, but both of us were moving fast when we were not at our respective warehouses.

I remember one weekend Rosalynn and I agreed to serve some papers on Homer personally. When we went by his warehouse, one of his employees said he had just gone home for supper. We went to his home, a nice white clapboard house adjacent to a rarely used railroad spur line. When I knocked on the front door, we heard him say, "Come in!" Inside, we found Homer sitting in an easy chair, dressed in silk pajamas and with a tray of food on his lap. He was watching television while he ate. He didn't get up but welcomed us with a smile and accepted the summons or whatever it was we had to deliver. We thanked him and left.

Throughout this hectic two-week period, he and I went out of our way both in person and in our frequent public statements to compliment each other and to profess our friendship and mutual respect. I never have believed that Homer was in any way implicated in the fraudulent activities in Georgetown that day.

✯ ✯ ✯

Six days after the election, on Monday, October 22, the *Atlanta Journal* ran a prominent front-page story on the disputed senatorial race in the Fourteenth District, the first dispatch from John Pennington. Although the article did not break much ground beyond what we already knew—it was based almost exclusively on Pennington's interview with me—at least readers in the entire state could now know the background of our Senate primary race. The article also reported the allegation that "every election law on the books" had been violated in Quitman County, including ballot box stuffing. There was a description of what had happened in the courthouse while people were trying to vote, an account of the disparity between ballots counted and votes cast, and a statement that Senator Robert McKenzie had observed the same events. Since the newspaper did at least partially live up to its claim that "the *Journal* covers Dixie like the dew," the story precipitated renewed interest in southwest Georgia. The *Americus Times-Recorder* and a few other news media had been sent copies of our recount petition, and from then on we were able to have our legal actions and evidence publicized.

The next day several newspapers reported on the contents of the individual affidavits that we had filed and made public, beginning with lengthy quotations from the statements of John Pope and Ralph Balkcom.

These first reports were supplemented by statements

from a few Georgetown voters. W. N. Roberts, a Quitman County farmer, said, "There was no secret place provided for voting and the whole place for voting was no more than 6 feet by 6 feet and it was impossible for more than one or two people to vote at one time and that any one in the room could witness this vote."

Durwood Graddy, a local mechanic and car salesman, swore that "the place provided for voting was over a counter with no way possible to cast your vote in secrecy. The ballot box had a hole in the top large enough to put my fist in it. I would like to be able to vote a secret ballot and would like to have our elections carried out in a lawful, impartial manner which we did not have on this date."

Mrs. Henry L. Balkcom, Jr., whose husband was a county commissioner and Ralph's second cousin, said that when she cast her ballot, Joe Hurst told her, "This is the man who is going to win," and pointed to a Homer Moore campaign card.

Doc Hammond was quoted in the *Times-Recorder* as saying that it was only the second time he had ever held an election and he was not very familiar with the election laws. He also claimed he tried to influence only one voter as poll manager for that day.

John Pope refuted this statement. He had personally seen Hammond try to tell at least one hundred people how to vote. John added, "While watching the votes being counted I saw the clerk remove at one time, all folded together in one bundle, as many as eight ballots, They were all for Homer Moore."

Our case would have been lost without this statewide publicity. Now it was assuming a life of its own, and there was no doubt that top officials in Georgia were becoming acquainted with it. We could see that political influence was going to be significant if the contest boiled down to a close call in interpreting the laws and Democratic party rules.

In later years, Warren Fortson remembered that "we needed a big gun since our case was shot through with politics," and the biggest gun we could find was Charles Kirbo.

Kirbo was the former law partner of Judge Griffin Bell, who had recommended him to us in part because he was from Bainbridge, in south Georgia, and knew the lay of the land. More important, he had represented Judge Tom Marshall in his recount dispute. On Wednesday, October 24, Warren called Charlie Kirbo at his office, and as soon as he expressed his willingness to talk to us, we got in the car and drove the three hours to Atlanta to tell him our story. I didn't even go by Plains to change clothes. But the more Warren and I talked about it on the way up, the less likely it seemed that we could win our case. We were somewhat doubtful when we arrived at his fancy office that this Atlanta lawyer would even be willing to hear us out.

We must have made quite a pair, Warren and I. The office of Kirbo's firm, King and Spalding, was the largest and probably the most ornate in Atlanta, more accustomed to the presence of business executives, high government officials, and statehouse lobbyists. I was wearing my ordinary work clothes, and even though Warren was a member of the Georgia bar, he was not much better dressed that day. I found out later that one of Kirbo's junior partners, David Gambrell, described the meeting this way: "In those days, at that firm, when meeting a new client, we were accustomed to seeing bold-looking men in business suits with recently polished shoes. On that occasion, the 'new client' in Charlie's office was a somewhat subdued looking person, dressed in khaki shirt and pants, wearing brogans or something close to it. He appeared to have just climbed off of a tractor, or to have spent the early part of the day at a peanut warehouse, or some other place where a dust mask would have been suitable attire."

Warren and I, however, had more important things on our minds than sartorial assessments when we were ushered into Kirbo's office that afternoon. We told him what had happened at the courthouse in Georgetown on primary day and brought him up to date on our investigations and interviews. He listened sympathetically and made the noncommittal statement that he was impressed with our tenacity in pursuing the case. What he didn't tell us—at least not then—was how slim were our chances of success. Unlike Tom Marshall's relatively simple election dispute, our allegations were harder to prove. Kirbo also knew that Joe Hurst would surely pull every string possible to make sure he had a witness of his own for every witness of ours.

Kirbo's other reservations centered on Judge Crow. I had never heard of the judge, but Kirbo had practiced before him when he lived in Bainbridge and described him as honest but tough. Crow was quite conservative in his political philosophy and didn't like to waste time with frivolous arguments; in fact, he had never overturned an election on the basis of fraud. There was little room for maneuvering, for, as David Gambrell told us, the election law gave Judge

Crow a tremendous amount of power, and if he didn't like us or our politics, we might be sunk regardless of the evidence.

It seems clear, as I look back, that Kirbo and Gambrell didn't think we had much chance to win the case. However, the case was already making front-page headlines in the Atlanta newspapers, and they saw it as challenging and intriguing, particularly in the new political climate in Georgia. Kirbo decided to take our case, and Gambrell would assist him. None of us had the slightest idea what Judge Crow might do. Charlie Kirbo admitted as much in later years, saying, "Really, I knew we didn't have much chance. There was no skill involved in the legal outcome, just luck."

We also realized that the state Democratic officials had very little interest in our case. It had been obvious at the state convention that we were just a distant blip on their radar screen, best ignored. It was unlikely that any reasonable decision by the local officials would be reversed. Following implementation of the "one man, one vote" ruling, Carl Sanders had won a remarkable victory in the governor's race on his acceptance of an end to the county unit system and his promise to clean out the old political bosses. The people's first experience with the direct popular vote for governor had been very positive, even in the smaller counties. But enough of the old system survived to snuff out our challenge to Joe Hurst's electoral fraud unless we could manage to win our election fight in both the legal and political arenas.

Although we counted on Charlie Kirbo and his Atlanta law firm to make sure we didn't overlook some key factor at the state Democratic party level, we had put most of our faith in the news coverage that would build interest and support in our contest. As the week drew to a close, stories continued to appear in our local newspapers (mainly repeating the facts that were already known), but, to our disappointment, John Pennington seemed to have lost interest in the case. His Monday and Tuesday articles had not gone beyond what we had told him the previous Friday, plus what was in a few of the affidavits. On Wednesday and Thursday we waited for the Atlanta newspapers and searched them eagerly. Not a word.

On Friday, October 26, I received a petition signed by more than 10 percent of Quitman County's registered voters, stating that voting in the Senate race and prior contests had been conducted in a manner that prevented the holding of "fair and impartial elections." The petitioners asked me to continue my efforts to expose the illicit voting practices and help them clean up politics in their county. We added this petition to the affidavits to further strengthen our case.

Also that day, John Pennington's front-page story in the *Journal* hit like a bombshell. We knew he had been talking to some of the Quitman County people and digging around in the courthouse files, but Mrs. Ina Graddy, the clerk of the court, had let it be known that he seemed more interested in the statewide primary voting in September. In fact, his article concentrated on the lieutenant governor's runoff election, not ours. We found this very disappointing, not realizing at the time that there was no documentary evidence at all from the public records about voters' names or how they cast ballots in my race.

Pennington's story, datelined Georgetown, Georgia,

pulled no punches. His opening words were "The state-wide Democratic primaries held in this Southwest Georgia town in September were conducted with no apparent regard for the law." He went on to report that lists of those who voted in the primary and runoff elections contained the names of people who could not possibly have voted, including those who were dead or in the federal penitentiary.

He named J. C. Hollingsworth, who had died several months earlier but came back to vote number 109 in the first election and then 303 in the runoff. Hollingsworth also brought to the polls his son, who had been away in military service for several years. Lloyd Hovey, who had lost his citizen's rights because he was then serving his second sentence in Kilby prison in Alabama for felony offenses, was the seventy-first person to vote on September 26. A number of citizens of Quitman County who lived far away had voted in the runoff election for lieutenant governor, although they had not returned for a visit and no absentee ballots were counted in that election. Several people were listed as having voted twice.

Most newsworthy was how carefully people in Quitman County had arranged themselves to vote. The records showed that "numerous large family groups, some of them construction workers who have left Georgetown, are listed as having voted in the order in which they appear on the voters' lists." Furthermore, beginning with voter number 30, "a hundred and seventeen people, out of a total vote of 733, are listed as having lined up and cast their ballots in alphabetical order, even down to the second and third letters of the last name."

A particularly interesting voter was Georgia Ruth

Williams, who voted number 302 in the runoff election, just ahead of the late Mr. Hollingsworth. In the first election, she had chosen her associates more carefully, voting number 264 just after a Ward, a Watson, six Whitakers, and a Whitman and in front of a Worthy and two Wrights. Contacted by telephone where she lived in California, Ms. Williams stated that she had not been in Quitman County in several years and had never cast an absentee ballot.

Pennington had photographed the election records and had interviewed Joe Hurst, his associates, and a number of the people who had been falsely listed as having voted. It was a devastating report about Georgetown voting, and he went on to tie it in to our case. "This is the same precinct from which Jimmy Carter, a senatorial candidate from Plains in the recent special election for the reapportioned Senate, contested his defeat by 139 votes, charging a violation of every election law on the books in the Georgetown primary."

The *Atlanta Journal*'s editorial cartoon (published on Halloween) showed a Quitman County official caught in the act of copying names off gravestones onto blank ballots. The cartoon's caption was a quotation from Macbeth, warning against "supernatural soliciting." The *Atlanta Constitution*'s cartoon was even more pointed, depicting a Quitman County politician campaigning in a cemetery, saying, "And I owe it all to you, my public-spirited friends."

In rebuttal to these charges, Joe Hurst was quoted as saying it was not possible that the names of any unqualified persons could be listed as voting. Referring to one of the dead men, he said: "His name may be on the voting list, but he damn sure didn't vote. I don't think so anyway. I didn't hold the polls. I don't think our poll managers would let a dead person vote. I know they wouldn't."

Strangely, Pennington reported, there were no absentee ballots in the runoff for lieutenant governor but about 200 in the governor's race. This was nearly a fourth of the total voter registration of 831. Only 90 registered voters failed to cast ballots in the governor's election, a remarkable demonstration of good citizenship, since many of the people had long ago moved out of the county. Questioned about the fact that people from California, Virginia, and Washington had been listed as voting when they had not returned to the county and there were no absentee ballots, Hurst replied that Mrs. Elton Friedman, the clerk of the Board of Registrars, had handled the lists of voters. She, in turn, said, "I gave them to Daddy and them," meaning the members of the Board of Registrars. Her father, Loren Whitaker, and all the board members denied knowing anything about missing absentee ballots, and Whitaker—who ten days earlier had pleaded with John Pope to help keep his daughter out of the public eye—added that it was not the business of any "outsider" to see any of the Quitman County records.

Finally, Pennington mentioned the overwhelming victories of Hurst's favorite candidate in these tainted elections. Despite an impressive statewide majority, Carl Sanders polled only 79 votes in Quitman County, while his opponent, Marvin Griffin, received 649. Peter Zack Geer, in whose runoff election Pennington had found his examples of fraud, won by more than a ten-to-one-decision. A familiar pattern was taking shape before the public's eyes.

chapter 6

★★★★★★★★★★★★★★★★★★★★★★★★★★★★★★

"We'll Always Drink Old Crow"

The Quitman County Democratic Executive Committee chairman, the redoubtable Joe Hurst, scheduled an official hearing for Monday, October 29, to consider allegations of impropriety in the Senate election in Georgetown. Ralph Balkcom and the Garys confirmed what we had already suspected: although the committee members were elected in relatively open elections, Hurst had always been able to maintain at least a majority of the votes.

We were to meet in the county courthouse, along with Homer Moore and his lawyers, to present our case and hear counterarguments. The committee would then make its judgment. In the week prior to this hearing, Homer had expanded his legal defense to match our addition of Charles

Kirbo. Joining Jesse Bowles was George Busbee, a state representative from Albany who was well connected in the state capital. Most important for Homer, Busbee was close to gubernatorial nominee Carl Sanders, who would have to approve the final decision of the state Democratic party.

Warren Fortson and I had done most of the preparation for this hearing, with Kirbo staying in Atlanta and getting ready for the recount before Judge Crow, which had now been scheduled for Thursday, November 1, just five days before the general election. We had done everything possible to get ready, completing as many sworn affidavits as we could get. After the *Atlanta Journal* articles were published, we found the Quitman County people more willing to give us their sworn testimony in writing. The crucial issue would be this: if the Georgetown box was counted, Homer Moore would be the winner; if the box was thrown out, I would be the state senator.

Now, in the hearing before the Quitman County committee, our strategy was molded by the hopelessness of having Joe Hurst and his associates admit their own guilt. We had secured a solid file of sworn statements that proved the violation of almost every provision in the Georgia election code. Many of the citizens had agreed to testify publicly, so that the Quitman County people and the assembled news reporters could be presented with proof that the election had been completely fraudulent. Publicity was what we wanted, while laying a foundation for later appeals to the state Democratic committee or to the state courts. At least we would get our best case on the record.

★★★

★ *133*

But as things turned out, we never got a chance. At 10:00 A.M., Homer and I arrived at the courthouse in Georgetown with our lawyers. About fifty people, mostly residents of Quitman County, had gathered to observe the proceedings. They were joined by several reporters, including John Pennington, who was now famous in the area. As chairman of the Quitman County Democratic Executive Committee, Joe Hurst presided, and the other members hearing our case were Frank Perkins, Pete Hammond, Mrs. Walter Lee Graddy, and Mac Greene.

These people were all well known to us. Early in the campaign, Ralph Balkcom and I had visited Frank Perkins, who was a county commissioner and who had promised to vote for me in the election. Pete Hammond, Doc's uncle, was the county road foreman, responsible for maintaining the dirt roads. He owed his job to Henry Balkcom, chairman of the county commissioners, who was Ralph's cousin and my strong supporter. Mrs. Graddy's husband had a state job, working at the Factory for the Blind in Bainbridge. Joe Hurst had gone out of his way to get the job for him, and the Graddys knew that Hurst could as easily have him fired. Mac Greene usually supported Joe's proposals in the Democratic committee, so we had little hope that he might vote our way, even though he had promised to vote for me in the primary and may have done so. We knew that he had a good working relationship with Hurst and was under a lot of pressure concerning his decision at the hearing. In fact, Ralph told us that Hurst had pulled out all stops in preparing for this supreme test of political power in his community. No matter what evidence was presented to the committee members at the hearing,

Ernest Vandiver, governor of Georgia in 1962. (Courtesy, Georgia Department of Archives and History.)

State Senator Carl Sanders, campaigning for governor, June 1962. (Reprinted with permission from the *Atlanta Journal* and the *Atlanta Constitution*.)

Judge Griffin Bell of the United States Court of Appeals for the Fifth Circuit. Judge Bell sat on both judicial panels that met in the spring of 1962 to rule on the legality of Georgia's county unit system; his opinion in *Sanders v. Gray* declared it unconstitutional. He later served as attorney general of the United States. (Courtesy, Mercer University.)

JIMMY
CARTER

FOR STATE
SENATOR

With only fifteen days to campaign (at the height of the harvest season), I had neither the time nor the campaign workers to blanket the district with billboards or literature. I personally nailed posters like this on trees and posts at the major road crossings of the Fourteenth District. (Courtesy, Jimmy Carter Library.)

VOTE FOR

JIMMY CARTER

CANDIDATE FOR

State Senator

PRIMARY OCTOBER 16th, 1962

Your Vote and Support Will Be Appreciated

One of my campaign cards for the October 16 Senate primary. (Courtesy, Jimmy Carter Library.)

VOTE FOR

JIMMY CARTER

JIMMY CARTER

CANDIDATE FOR

STATE SENATOR

PRIMARY OCT. 16th, 1962

QUALIFICATIONS

EDUCATION—Graduated from Annapolis after attending Plains High School, Ga. Southwestern College and Ga. Tech. Member of Sumter County Board of Education for 6 years and now serving as chairman.

BUSINESS—Manager and partner in Plains of a warehouse, peanut sheller and cotton gin business.

FARMING—A farmer in Webster and Sumter counties, grower of Certified Seed Peanuts--Active in state farm organizations, Director of Foundation Seeds Inc., past president of Ga. Crop Improvement Association.

PERSONAL—Native of Plains; 38 years old; married to Rosalynn Smith of Plains; father of 3 sons; Baptist; former Deputy District Governor of Lions International; officer in U.S. Navy Submarine force for 7 years.

This advertisement paid for by The Carter-For-Senate Committee

This advertisement ran in the *Americus Times-Recorder* shortly before the election. (Courtesy, Jimmy Carter Library.)

Homer Moore, my opponent for the Democratic nomination for the Georgia State Senate. (Courtesy, Jimmy Carter Library.)

Sam Singer, state representative from Stewart County, was Homer Moore's campaign manager in the 1962 Senate race. (Courtesy, Georgia Department of Archives and History.)

Joe Hurst, state representative and political boss of Quitman County, at work in the legislature, 1962. (Reprinted with permission from the *Atlanta Journal* and the *Atlanta Constitution*.)

Rosalynn's cousin Ralph Balkcom, the Quitman County school superintendent, who alerted us to the fact that Joe Hurst was interfering with the free conduct of the Senate election in Georgetown. (Courtesy, Theresa D. Balkcom.)

The Quitman County Court House in Georgetown, where the disputed election took place. This photo was taken on one of my many trips to Georgetown in the aftermath of the primary; I am seen pacing with my head down, fourth from the right. (Courtesy, *The Washington Post.* Reprinted with permission of Marilyn Pennington.)

My friend John Pope, who witnessed the voting irregularities in Georgetown on Primary Day. (Reprinted with permission from the *Atlanta Journal* and the *Atlanta Constitution.*)

Carter Says Will Request Vote Recount

PLAINS, Ga. — A recount will be asked in the 14th Senatorial District primary vote held Tuesday in seven Chattahoochee Valley counties, according to the loser.

Jimmy Carter, Plains, told The Enquirer Wednesday night that he will ask for a recount. He said the counties in which he will petition for a recount will be decided on today.

The complete but unofficial vote in the district gave Carter 139 votes less than Homer Moore of Richland.

In the unofficial returns, Moore led Carter in five of the seven counties in the new senatorial district. Moore led in Stewart, Webster, Quitman, Randolph and Terrell Counties.

The other two counties in the district are Sumpter and Chattahoochee.

Irregularities Charged by Carter; Recount Requested in Georgetown

By RUDY HAYES
Enquirer Correspondent

AMERICUS, Ga. — Jimmy Carter, candidate for state senator from the 14th Senatorial District, said Monday that a recount of the Georgetown box of Quitman County may show him to be winner by about 75 votes instead of a loser by 139 votes.

A petition prepared by Americus attorney Warren Fortson for Carter, has been filed with members of the Quitman County Democratic Executive Committee. The petition calls for either a recount or the throwing out of the ballot box.

The Quitman County Committee has until Oct. 30 to answer. Carter said Monday that if the Quitman County Committee rules against him, he will appeal to the State Democratic Executive Committee.

The recount request has been filed in connection with the special Democratic primary for state senator. Homer Moore, Richland businessman, was apparent winner by 139 votes according to the returns.

Included in the charges of irregularities listed in the petition for recount was the accusation that no provisions were made for a "secret ballot" at the Georgetown box.

The petition also contends that the ballot box was made of cardboard with a large hole in the top, which was large enough to permit easy withdrawal of ballots after they were inserted.

The 38-year-old Plains warehouse owner and cotton ginner, said he is lodging the protest at the request of numerous Quitman County citizens who told him violations occurred during last Tuesday's vote.

He said he holds more than 30 affidavits from Quitman citizens attesting to alleged irregularities they witnessed.

Members of the Quitman Democratic Executive Committee include Joe Hurst, a state representative and an employee of the State Agriculture Department, Frank Perkins, Pete Hammond, Mrs. A. L. Graddy, and Mac Greene.

Carter charges that "repeatedly during the day voters were harangued by the election officials while marking ballots, being urged to vote for Homer Moore. Voters were told that Homer Moore was a home county man and that he already had won the senate office once before, that the election officials had voted for Moore and that they should do likewise."

The Sumter Countian further alleges that a "Homer Moore campaign card was kept displayed at all times on the small counter where ballots were marked. Election officials frequently talked to them all the way into the office of the ordinary about whom to vote for, and then watched closely as the voters marked ballots.

'Elect Us A Senator'

He said a remark frequently used by election officials was, "We have got to elect us a senator."

Carter also said that on two occasions while present he asked that voters be provided a secret voting place and the request was refused.

He also asked that voters be left alone and no attempt be made to persuade persons to vote for Homer Moore while they were marking ballots.

Carter said one official replied, "Voters didn't pay much attention to him and he knew how they were going to vote anyhow."

It is further alleged that only 333 ballot stubs were torn off the pad used in the election, but there were 420 ballots in the box when counted. Only 410 names were reported listed on the voter's tabulation sheet. There were no absentee ballots cast.

Other Alleged Violations

Articles that appeared in the local newspapers after I requested a recount of the vote in Georgetown. (Courtesy, Jimmy Carter Library.)

John Pennington, the *Atlanta Journal* reporter whose stories helped to expose the fraud in the election. (Reprinted with permission from the *Atlanta Journal* and the *Atlanta Constitution*.)

. . . And I Owe It All to You, My Public-Spirited Friends . .

'THIS SUPERNATURAL SOLICITING CANNOT BE ILL . . . CANNOT BE GOOD.'—MACBETH

Oct 31, 1962 Atlanta Journal

These editorial cartoons appeared in the *Atlanta Constitution (left)* and the *Atlanta Journal* at the height of the controversy over the Georgetown ballot box. (Reprinted with permission from the *Atlanta Journal* and the *Atlanta Constitution*.)

Warren Fortson *(second from right)*, a longtime friend of the family and my most trusted adviser during the election controversy, seen here examining some papers during one of our fact-finding trips to Quitman County. I am at the far left of the photograph, and Ralph Balkcom is at the far right. (Courtesy, *St. Petersburg Times*. Reprinted with permission of Marilyn Pennington.)

Charles Kirbo, the influential Atlanta attorney who agreed to take my case in the election dispute, seen here a few years earlier with his son, Charles Jr. (Courtesy, Charles Kirbo.)

George Busbee, state representative from Dougherty County, who served on Homer Moore's legal team in the election dispute. In 1974, he would be elected governor of Georgia. (Courtesy, Georgia Department of Archives and History.)

Here I am trying to make a point to Joe Hurst at the height of the controversy over the disposition of the election. He seems to want to have as little to do with me as possible. (Courtesy, *The Washington Post*. Reprinted with permission of Marilyn Pennington.)

The general election victory, as reported in the *Americus Times-Recorder* on November 7, 1962. (Courtesy, Jimmy Carter Library.)

Judge Tom Marshall, who heard the final appeal of our case on the eve of the general election. He later served as chief justice of the Georgia Supreme Court. (Courtesy, Georgia Department of Archives and History.)

Voters Give Carter Mar[g]in
Of 831 Votes for Senate

Voters gave Jimmy Carter of Plains a resounding 831-vote majority over opponent Homer Moore in balloting for the 14th District Senatorial seat in Tuesday's general election.

Returns from all 45 precincts in the 7-county district showed 3,013 votes for Carter and 2,182 for Richland's Moore.

However, the condition remained clouded in the topsy-turvy race and it was conceivable that candidate Moore might contest the results.

Mr. Moore told The Times-Recorder Wednesday that he planned to confer with his attorneys during the afternoon and his decision on whether to file a protest would be made at that session.

Superior Court Judge Tom Marshall, Americus, ruled at a hearing Monday night that there was no qualified candidate for the 14th District seat and instructed ordinaries of the seven counties involved to remove Carter's name from the ballot.

Two days before the State Democratic Committee had ruled that Moore's name be removed from the ticket and that of Carter's substituted following a recount of the Georgetown precinct where alleged irregularities had occurred. The recount had reversed the outcome of the Oct. 16 primary and made Carter winner by 65 votes over Moore.

However, because there were only hours remaining before the election, two counties were unable to comply with the order by Marshall. Therefore, Carter's name appeared on the official ballot in Sumter and Quitman counties, while no candidate was listed in the remaining five over the district. Thus, all of the votes received by Moore Tuesday were write-ins, and for Carter as well, except in Sumter and Quitman.

Carter carried four counties of the seven, including the heavy Sumter vote. Moore took the remaining three.

Here is a breakdown of the vot-
(Continued On Page Four)

VOTERS GIVE

ing in the district.

Counties for Carter: Sumter, 1399 to 352; Quitman, 448 to 23; Chattahoochee, 73 to 68; Randolph 358 to 320.

Counties for Moore: Webster, 276 to 102; Stewart, 666 to 248; and Terrell, 477 to 385.

In Sumter County Mr. Carter took all nine precincts as follows:

27th District (City of Americus), 941 to 183; 15th (Leslie), 94 to 92; Old 16th (Huntington, 14 to 13; New 16th (Sumter City), 35 to 4; 17th (Thompson), 44 to 4; Old 26th (Plains), 201 to 28; New 26th (Concord), 24 to 12; 28th (Chambliss), 15 to 11; and 29th (Andersonville), 31 to 0.

Quitman County, where the alleged voting irregularities occurred in the Oct. 16 primary, gave Carter dramatic support. 448 to only 23 for Moore. First results in the first election gave Moore 360 votes to 136 for Carter.

Carter's home county of Sumter turned out to give him an overwhelming margin. Combined returns in the other six counties had Moore ahead 1830 to 1614, but the Sumter vote pushed Carter far into the lead.

Marshall said he would take no action against officials in the counties which failed to remove Carter's name from the ballot unless charges were brought before him.

"I am not an enforcement officer," Marshall said. "Any further action will have to come from one of the parties involved in the suit."

TO TH[E]
OF SUM[TER]

From the bott[om]

thank you all f[or]

you gave me in [the elec-]

tion.

Your kindnes[s]

spire me to my [best]

Peter Zack Geer *(left)* was elected lieutenant governor in 1962. He is shown here being sworn in to his previous post as executive secretary to Governor Vandiver. At right is George D. Stewart, executive secretary of the Georgia Democratic party. (Reprinted with permission from the *Atlanta Journal* and the *Atlanta Constitution*.)

My cousin Perry Gordy *(right)*, the newly elected senator from the fifteenth district, accompanying me into the Senate chamber on the first day of the legislative session, January 15, 1963. Visible over my right shoulder is Leroy Johnson, Georgia's first black state senator since Reconstruction. (Reprinted with permission of the *Columbus Ledger-Enquirer*.)

A state senator at last, taking the oath of office. I am fifth from the right.
(Reprinted with permission of the *Columbus Ledger-Enquirer*.)

jobs and future political careers would likely shape their decision.

Warren was permitted to speak first, but after he had spoken just a minute or two outlining the legal basis for the hearing, Hurst called on Homer Moore's team to respond. Jesse Bowles stood and stated that we had not established a cause for action and that the law and Democratic party rules gave the local committee the final authority to make a decision on any contested election. He then asked that our action be declared invalid and sat down. Immediately, Chairman Hurst called a recess and the committee left the room. No evidence or testimony had been presented.

During this brief recess, Warren and I double-checked our case just to make sure we had all the affidavits in the same order as his presentation. Our general plan was to proceed methodically from one section of the Georgia election code to the next, proving by affidavits and direct testimony that our allegations were true. About half the people who had given us the sworn statements were present at the hearing and were willing to substantiate their experiences before the committee.

Warren went outside the courtroom to talk to one of our witnesses, and Rosalynn and I stayed inside just to keep an eye on our documents. After the committee members had been gone for not more than two or three minutes, they strolled back into the courtroom. Four of the members took their seats, and Joe Hurst walked over to Jesse Bowles and Homer Moore. I overheard him say, "We sustained your motion." I could hardly believe what I had heard and ran outside to tell Warren.

When we returned to the courtroom, Joe and the other

committee members were preparing to leave. Rosalynn, Warren, I, and our Quitman County supporters were dismayed and angry. Warren was particularly furious and demanded that the group be reassembled. With a smile, Joe complied with this request and reconvened the meeting. Then he simply said, "We have made a decision."

Warren almost shouted, "How is anybody supposed to know what is going on?"

Joe replied, "We sustained the motion of the defendant."

"Are you refusing to hear the contest at all?"

"Yeah."

We hadn't expected any help from the committee, but we had, perhaps foolishly, never considered that our evidence would not even be heard and entered into the official records. Joe Hurst, however, had completely outflanked us. By not letting Warren present our evidence, he not only cleared the way for his committee to dismiss our challenge but also made it virtually impossible for us to appeal the decision. Under Democratic party rules, a county committee could be overruled only if the evidence on record was considered an insufficient basis for the decision rendered. Joe knew quite well that if there was no evidence favorable to me on the record, I would have no grounds on which to challenge the Quitman County committee's judgment.

Warren and I talked a few seconds, not knowing what to do, and finally decided to ask that the committee members be polled. After some hesitation, Hurst agreed, and the five Democratic officials gave their verdict. Joe indicated which one would speak first, just asking whether they agreed or disagreed with the committee decision.

MAC GREENE: "I agree."

MRS. GRADDY: "I agree."

PETE HAMMOND: "I didn't vote."

FRANK PERKINS: "I also abstained."

Then Joe waited a short while and said, "I agree with the decision."

Warren then made a short statement, saying that many of the state's election laws had been openly flouted and that we had brought the evidence to prove this charge. He added that the best way to handle this case was to let the decision be made in Quitman County, among the people who were most seriously affected by the illegal practices. When Warren added that the contents of the ballot box would be the best evidence on which the committee could make a sound judgment and demanded that it be brought forth, Joe stood up and said, "This meeting is adjourned."

To emphasize the finality of their rejection of the fraud charges, three of the committee members left the courtroom, followed quickly by Homer Moore, Jesse Bowles, and Homer's supporters. Most of our group stayed in the room and gathered around Warren and me. They expressed consternation at what had happened, and many of them urged us not to give up our efforts. I realized that their concerns were not so much about the outcome of this particular race, which had obviously become a secondary matter, but about publicly exposing and putting an end to what had been going on for a long time in Quitman County.

I thought it was probably all over but tried to think of

something to say that would not be a final concession of defeat. Ralph Balkcom remembered my exact words: "You people have no control of things in your own county. You've lost control of your own affairs. It looks like I've lost too, but if you will help me, I'll fight this to the end. If you're not willing to get involved, I can't do anything. If you won't help, I'll just pack up all I have and go back to Plains." After my Quitman County supporters promised not to yield, there was really not much else for us to say. I promised that we would be back in Georgetown Thursday to continue with our recount petition.

But all of us who had become familiar with the election laws realized that our main hope had been in pursuing the contest on the basis of fraud. We were convinced that the recount would be just that—a straightforward examination of individual ballots and then a tabulation of those that looked all right.

On the way back home, Warren mentioned the possibility of taking our case to a federal court, but this was unlikely because no federal offices had been involved in our special election, as had been the case in the September 12 primary, when a U.S. congressman and senator had been nominated. There was always the possibility of appealing this decision, but the laws seemed quite clear that any higher court or legal body could review only one issue: whether proper procedures had been followed in the lower body. Only evidence that had not been available during the first hearing could be considered on appeal.

Privately, Warren and I were concerned about a strange court ruling on which Jesse Bowles had based his argument before Joe Hurst's panel. This decision, rendered in the 1940s, had stated that final decisions over electoral procedure rested solely with the county committee, regardless of whether the state committee had made a contrary ruling. (Apparently, in that case the court had sought to prevent a remote and possibly biased state Democratic committee in Atlanta from overriding a more responsible and more knowledgeable group of local officials.) Warren's contention, as presented in his brief remarks after Hurst had announced the committee's peremptory decision, was that this ruling had been superseded by the Democratic party rules adopted in April 1962, which stated explicitly that

> any party to a contest who is dissatisfied with the determination of the County Executive Committee may appeal in writing to the State Executive Committee. . . . Said contest shall be heard and decided by the Contest Committee named by the State Chairman. The appeal shall be heard upon the evidence submitted to the County Executive Committee and *no new evidence shall be submitted to the Committee except newly discovered evidence* [emphasis added]. . . . When the contest is determined the result of its determination shall be certified to the Chairman of the County Executive Committee, where the contest originated. The finding of the Contest Committee on such contest shall in all cases be final and conclusive.

This sounded good, but there was an obvious problem in that Joe Hurst had made sure that no evidence was presented to the county executive committee.

When we realized that John Pennington had stayed inside the courthouse and was listening to our excited discussion, most of the attention shifted to him. The key anti-Hurst people in the county had gotten to know Pennington well, and his news articles had, so far, been the most exciting and significant developments in a long time. The Americus, Columbus, and Atlanta newspapers gave an accurate report the next day on what had happened, along with our announcement of plans to appeal the Quitman County ruling. Luke Teasley's article in nearby Columbus ran on page 9, but Pennington's much fuller report was a major front-page story in the *Atlanta Journal*, along with the following editorial, headlined "Cloud over Georgetown":

> The hearing that was supposed to inquire into charges of voting irregularities in Quitman County was a miserable flop.
>
> It lasted for only a few minutes and those in charge didn't even bother to hear the evidence, even though some 30 affidavits of alleged lawbreaking were ready for presentation.
>
> They acted as if they didn't even want to begin an investigation. In effect, the Democratic Party officials of Quitman County walked away from the voting mess that they had every reason to investigate on the basis of what had been brought out previously, including an independent check by an Atlanta Journal reporter.
>
> The attorney representing the candidate who asked that the Georgetown box be thrown out because virtually every election law on the books had been violated, including voting of the dead, said the quick decision reached by local authorities would be appealed to the State Democratic Committee.

There's every reason why it should be.

Certainly there ought to be an opportunity for airing this smelly situation and reaching a verdict on the basis of facts and evidence rather than personal politics.

It seems a shame that such conditions should leave a stain on this state at a time when it's trying to get some semblance of fairness into its system of voting and representation.

Georgians shouldn't rest until they're convinced a more determined effort is made to remove the voting cloud that hangs low over Georgetown.

That afternoon in Atlanta, U.S. Attorney Charles Goodson said that the federal government was interested in vote fraud in any primary or general election among candidates for federal office. That would include the September 12 primary in Georgetown that John Pennington had exposed as fraudulent. When asked about this statement, Joe Ray, the prosecuting attorney in Quitman County's judicial circuit and Joe Hurst's close friend, replied that any election irregularities had to "address themselves to the Quitman County grand jury." But the next grand jury would not convene until March 1963. Furthermore, the judge of the district was Walter I. Geer, the uncle of Peter Zack Geer, who had received such an overwhelming vote in Quitman County in the September primary for lieutenant governor. It had been on his behalf that Joe Hurst had lined up the dead, imprisoned, and other absent voters to mark their ballots.

***

It was now Tuesday, October 30, and our time was running out. Every passing day was filled with more activity than the day before. Immediately after the Quitman County committee refused to hear our allegations, Charles Kirbo helped us file an appeal with the state Democratic executive committee. He had been working with us, mostly from his office in Atlanta, where he had been concentrating almost exclusively on the official recount.

The new state Democratic party chairman, J. B. Fuqua, was the owner of major television and radio stations in and around Augusta, in northeast Georgia. An aggressive and brilliant businessman, Fuqua was known to be meticulously honest but a relative novice at politics. In addition to this new office, to which his friend Carl Sanders had appointed him, he had been nominated to fill Sanders's Senate seat.

However, the routine affairs of the Democratic party were still being handled by Executive Secretary George D. Stewart, whose reputation was just the opposite. We couldn't find him anywhere, and finally had to leave our appeal on his desk at the state Democratic office. Some lawyers in Kirbo's firm told us that George and his nephew Travis Stewart were big buddies of Sam Singer and that they might be off together—obviously not a good omen for our case. (Sam, for his part, had always denied being friendly with George Stewart. He did admit, however, that he had spent the previous weekend with Travis Stewart, who would soon succeed his uncle as executive secretary of the Democratic party.) There later came news reports that Stewart might rule on our appeal in two days, when he was expected to return to Atlanta. However, these reports were never confirmed.

✪✪✪

On Thursday morning, all of us assembled in Georgetown for the recount of election ballots. Judge Carl Crow
presided, flanked by Billy Horne and Sam Singer, the representatives of the two campaigns. Several hundred people
were packed into the courthouse, including a number of
my kinfolks and friends who had driven over from Sumter
County. Homer Moore had even more supporters with
him. Warren Fortson and Charlie Kirbo were there representing me, and Jesse Bowles and George Busbee were
Homer's lawyers.

My team and I had learned all we could about Judge
Carl Crow, because we knew that now my political future
was in his hands. Our knowledge, however, was superficial
—we found out only that he was honest, conservative,
nearing retirement age, favored brief statements in his
court, and was inclined to be irritable because he had just
given up smoking. The other people in the courtroom probably knew even less, because the law required that recount
referees not be from the judicial circuit within which the
recount was to take place, and Crow had never held court
anywhere near Georgetown. Charlie Kirbo related one an-
ecdote before the proceedings began, indicating at the very
least that Judge Crow anticipated an interesting event. A
couple of days before the recount, he had called the judge
on another matter, and Judge Crow had mentioned the
hearing on the Georgetown case. In a joking manner, Kirbo
had said, "Maybe I just as well not come all the way down
from Atlanta. My client doesn't have much money for
travel expenses." The judge replied, "You just as well come
on down."

I watched Judge Crow closely as he came into the courtroom and settled himself for the proceedings. He had requested in advance that a large spittoon be placed adjacent to his chair, and the first thing he did, before saying anything, was to cut off a large chew of tobacco and put it in his mouth. Chewing tobacco was much more prevalent in those days than now, and there were many techniques. Some people would chew tobacco all day without ever spitting. Judge Crow was at the opposite extreme, having just taken up the habit as a substitute for cigarettes, and he expelled a long stream of dark brown liquid every couple of minutes in the general direction of the spittoon. At these moments, no matter how important the testimony, it was difficult to maintain attention on whoever was speaking.

We were pleased to see that Judge Crow wanted first to understand how the election had been conducted. He made no effort to abbreviate the legal arguments or to prevent the introduction of evidence and testimony. His procedure was quite different from the narrowly restricted agenda in most recount hearings, so it was possible to show that the intent of large numbers of voters did not match the marked ballots in the box. No one knew if these revelations would be similar to those that John Pennington had reported in the runoff election for lieutenant governor.

Although the proceedings lacked some of the discipline of a formal trial, Judge Crow presided with authority and never hesitated to call down a lawyer or witness who began to wander away from the purpose. He seemed to be making a point of not showing any emotion or reacting to what he heard, so it was impossible for us to guess what he was thinking.

We called witnesses to back up the affidavits, but Homer's attorneys took a very passive stand. Their strategy seemed to be, first, to rely on Judge Crow's reluctance to invalidate ballots; second, to count on winning appeals down the line; or, finally, to assume that we would run out of time and Homer's victory would have to stand.

There were four hours of testimony from witnesses on both sides. Everyone agreed that a list of voters was kept and that ballots were torn from pads of numbered stubs. None of the Georgetown election officials, however, could remember under oath how many persons had voted, how many ballots had been used, or how many names had been listed. We all presumed that the contents of the box would answer all these questions. Furthermore, none of them admitted responsibility for sealing the ballot box, and they all claimed they didn't know who had.

Our witnesses confirmed what we had submitted in the affidavits, describing the absence of voting booths, being required to mark ballots with Doc Hammond and Joe Hurst watching closely, being encouraged or harassed to vote for Homer Moore, seeing Hurst examine ballots after they had been put in the ballot box, and Hurst's having been present when the votes were counted after the polls closed. Several people confirmed that there were packets of six to eight Homer Moore ballots folded together before they were separated to be counted, and that there were more ballots counted than there were people who voted.

Our first witness was Mrs. Ina Graddy, clerk of the superior court. She testified that Representative Joe Hurst turned the box over to her on the morning after the election, "but without filing the customary separate envelope containing tabulations, voters' list and the like." She said she "called his attention to the fact that the envelope was missing, and he said it was all inside the box." She pointed to the cardboard box on which she had written the vote tally for the entire county—360 Moore, 136 Carter—and "no envelope with consolidated returns and voters' list— 10-17-62."

Tom Gary provided some specific information that none of the poll workers could remember. He said he saw the voter list and only 333 people had voted when the polls closed at 7:00 P.M. on October 16. He stated, "After the count, Joe Hurst picked the stubs up and started out with them. He folded them over. I made this statement to him: 'Those stubs are supposed to go in the box, if I'm not mistaken.' He laid them back on the counter. That's where I read number 334 coming up."

Tommy added that when he voted, Mrs. Pace, the clerk, had told him there would be well over 400 ballots cast. He asked her why there would be that many when he was number 330 and it was closing time. He said that she had replied, "The absentees." He had then watched the ballots counted, and there were 410 names on the list of those who had voted and 420 ballots in box. He said Representative Hurst told him later there were no absentee ballots.

Mrs. Pace testified now that she knew nothing about any absentee ballots. She also could not remember whether the stubs and voter lists were put in the box with the ballots.

Loren Whitaker, chief poll manager, stated that he

was sick and away from the courthouse most of the day. He had returned for the counting of votes but didn't remember how many votes were cast and had no idea what happened to the ballot box and all the records that night.

Doc Hammond, who ran the polls most of the day, said he was the one who tore off ballots and handed them to people. He did not remember how many ballots were used and did not know what became of the voter records. He admitted that he had suggested to only one voter that she might prefer to vote against me and for Homer Moore. However, he went on to say that he picked up a sealed box from a chair at the courthouse and took it with him that night after the ballots had been counted.

Joe Hurst denied that he had observed the choice of voters or tried to influence anyone and claimed that all he knew about the election was that he had appointed the poll managers and had voted himself. He did state that "they handed me the box, already sealed" when the counting was completed. He couldn't recall who "they" were, except that "it was probably one of the election managers, Mr. Whitaker or Mrs. Barbaree, one." Then, he said, he had put the box on the chair from which Doc Hammond took it home.

Mrs. Bertha Barbaree had been the one who kept the list of voters during the day but said she did not know what happened to it later. She said the day ended with 410 names on the list. She had no idea how many ballots were used.

✯✯✯

It became obvious to everyone present that there could not be a reconciliation of all the conflicting testimony. It boiled down to the ballot box and what was in it. Kirbo had already reminded us that county bosses who habitually manipulated votes were experts on election laws and knew how to circumvent them to elect their candidates and how to cover their tracks. We knew that Hurst had been doing this for many years and was undoubtedly a master at concealing any illegal actions. It was quite likely that the ballot stubs, number of voters on the list, and the ballots counted would be in perfect agreement. After all, Joe and his people had had sixteen days to arrange the evidence.

From the very beginning of the hearing, the box had been sitting by itself on a table in front of Judge Crow and the two vote counters. Now the judge directed that it be opened, so the records could be examined and the ballots counted. My heart was in my throat. Since the witnesses had been talking about it so much, the box had become the center of attention. Depending on what one wanted or expected to see, it might have been holding some beautiful jewels or a large rattlesnake ready to strike. This was not the box that had been used instead of a voting booth but a much smaller one, with no hole cut in it. As far as we could see, the top was sealed neatly with plastic tape.

Judge Crow told the clerk to break the seal, but Billy Horne, our vote counter, said, "Judge, let's turn the box upside down." When this was done, we saw that the flaps were simply folded together, not sealed at all. We all watched Judge Crow, who didn't say a word or change his expression—but for a few seconds his jaw stopped moving.

When the box was opened, there was nothing inside except ballots. The stubs were gone, as was the list of voters who had gone to the polls that day. Most of the ballots were all mixed up, but a separate roll lay on top of the others, with a rubber band around it.

Judge Crow suggested that all the ballots be mixed together and counted, but Kirbo said, "No, let's keep them separate," which they did. There was not much of a hub-bub as the Georgetown ballots were counted, supposedly the 420 that had been reported on election night. Now, for some reason, there were 431 in the box, with 325 for Homer Moore and 106 for me. All of the rolled-up ballots had been marked for Homer Moore, and we could see right away that once this suspicious roll was included, there were far too many ballots for the number of people who had voted. For the first time we began to have some real hope.

Homer's lawyers didn't have much to say after the votes were counted, except that the ballots seemed to be in order and the tally agreed almost exactly with the returns that had been reported at the close of election day. According to them, the records that were missing were of secondary importance. Judge Crow did not ask them any questions but turned to see if we had any comment.

Kirbo stood up and began to talk. No one speaks more slowly than Charlie Kirbo. His words came out just two or three at a time, punctuated by long silent intervals, giving the impression that he doesn't quite understand his own subject. Later, we came to know that his mind works like a steel trap, but this was the first time we had seen him in a trial lawyer's role. At first I was disheartened, fearful that he would fumble away the potential advantage we had gained with the sterile records.

His legal argument seemed more like an intimate con-versation he might be having with Judge Crow as they walked around the edge of a south Georgia field behind a bird dog. He never raised his voice and there was no continuity or momentum to his sentences, so as he moved back and forth in the area in front of the bench and his head was turned away from us we had to lean forward to hear what he was saying.

He casually suggested that the Georgetown box ought to be thrown out entirely, because there was no way to tell what might have been in it if all the records had been kept. He knew that the judge had been in a lot of recounts before and wanted to do things exactly right so that the will of the voters might be expressed accurately in the results of any election. However, in this case something had happened to the stubs and voter list. He realized that, at the end of a hectic election day, no one could expect to see a perfect set of records. Things were done in a hurry, and people were tired and wanted to go home. Some mistakes might be inevitable in a situation like that.

He paused for quite a while, and walked back and forth as if he were wondering what he might say next. He stopped and began talking again in a much stronger and clearer voice.

"Judge, I'm not talking here in Georgetown about any honest mistakes or even some deliberate irregularities or illegalities. I'm talking about fraud. There is no way you can explain away the absence of all the stubs and all the voter lists. This is not an honest mistake. The Clerk has testified this morning that she asked Representative Hurst about the envelope, and he told her it was in the box. He's the Democratic Chairman and has been in government a long time. He's helped to run a lot of elections and knows the stubs and list have to be kept. He was standing there holding the box, and knew what was in it.

"Joe Hurst also knows that if you dispose of the stubs, and can't tell how many ballots were cast, it creates a problem. And Joe Hurst knows if you do away with the list of people who voted, you can't check the people who voted. Here, in this box, there is absolute evidence of fraud. No one can tell how the people in Georgetown voted, or even who voted.

"Judge, you and I come from the same part of the state, and we know something about chicken thieves. If somebody goes in a hen house in the middle of the night and puts a few of the chickens in a crocus sack and starts to walk away, they might pick up an old brush broom or something and kind of let it drag along behind them. Brooms are supposed to keep the yard clean, but it just happens that they also spoil out tracks if they drag behind somebody.

"The folks that were supposed to be protecting democracy here in Quitman County and letting the people choose their own leaders remind me of the fellow that went in the hen house. He knew what he was doing was wrong, taking somebody else's chickens, but he didn't want to get caught if the sheriff came and looked at his footprints the next day. This is what Mr. Hurst and his folks have done. They just spoiled out their tracks, after committing a crime against their own neighbors.

"Just a few minutes ago we saw a bunch of ballots all mixed up together that might possibly have represented what the people wanted, although we've had testimony that there were bunches of six or eight ballots folded up together in the box that night and all for the same man. But what about the big wad of ballots on top of the pile? There's no way that more than a hundred people in a row all voted for that same candidate. In this case, Judge, we're not asking that the thieves be punished, but just that they don't keep what they stole. We just request that their trumped up election returns not be used to decide who is going to represent the people of this county in the legislature.

"There's no way to tell about a single vote in that box. There's no listing of people that voted, and no other records in there."

Kirbo then addressed all three members of the recount panel: "It's not only your privilege, but your *duty* to straighten this out." He stood there awhile as though he was trying to think of what to say next and then walked back to his chair and sat down. Judge Crow did not react in any way but looked over at Homer's lawyers as if to see whether they had any response. They either shook their heads or didn't move, so the judge talked quietly for a few minutes with Sam Singer on one side and Billy Horne on the other. Then he announced that the recount hearing was adjourned for the day and that they would study the matter further.

Everyone was startled at what was in the box, but Judge Crow made no indication that he was particularly interested. Kirbo, however, suspected what was on the judge's mind.

On the way out of the courtroom, he told Judge Crow, "I know your normal practice, to just go by the count."

He replied, "Absolutely right."

"I never knew you to tolerate fraud, though."

"That bothers me."

"Ask your wife what she thinks," Kirbo said, as he and the judge parted ways.

Although he didn't know the people at all except for what he had seen or heard in the courtroom, Kirbo had figured out what had most likely happened on election night after the votes were counted. He surmised that Joe Hurst had told Doc Hammond to take the ballot box home and exchange the pack of ballots marked for Homer Moore for the same number of those marked for me. Then, in the wake of the uproar about fraud when the polls closed, Hammond may have gotten drunk or become confused about his orders. He probably put the Homer Moore ballots (still in a pack) into the box but failed to take out the correct number to keep the same overall total. It was an easy mistake to make. Then Hurst's people lost control of the ballot box, and all the ballots wound up this way in front of Judge Crow.

Sam Singer later confirmed this scenario when he asked Joe Hurst, "Why did y'all have to put a rubber band around that pile of ballots?"

Joe replied, "Well, we knew they were all for the same man, and we knew exactly how many there were, and we didn't want to have to count them twice."

We knew we were now in the final stages of our legal struggle and likely to move into the political arena. Whatever Judge Crow and the recount committee might rule, both sides were prepared to make a rapid appeal to the state Democratic executive committee. We were already looking at indications from Atlanta of what might happen. The *Atlanta Constitution* reported on Friday that Democratic Executive Secretary George Stewart, who had finally returned to his office, had said that I had a right to appeal to the state party under party rules, or that I could pursue legal action through the courts. He added that any action taken by the state party would have to come from the Contest Committee headed by Charles A. Pannell of Chatsworth. Pannell was unavailable to reporters for comment, and we had been unable to contact him ourselves.

The *Columbus Ledger*, in a page 13 news story about the opening of the box and the discovery that the voting records were missing, quoted a telephone interview with Pannell in which he said that he had been very busy campaigning for the state Senate himself and hadn't yet heard from George Stewart. It would be up to Pannell to call a meeting of his committee to consider any appeal. This article, referring to me as "Jerry Carter of the Plains community who lost to Homer Moore of Richland" and, assuming that I would lose the recount, stated that the Pannell committee would be the one to consider my appeal.

✻ ✻ ✻

Judge Crow announced late that afternoon that the recount decision would be made the next day, Friday, November 2. When the time came for the decision, we all assembled in the county courthouse in Albany, where the judge's chambers were. It was about the same crowd that had been in Quitman County the day before as far as our two groups of lawyers and close supporters were concerned, but only a few interested spectators had made the trip from Georgetown.

Although on previous occasions Homer and I had gone out of our way to exchange a handshake and a few pleasantries, this time we stayed on opposite sides of the courtroom. All of us were on pins and needles as Judge Crow, Billy Horne, and Sam Singer retired into what I assumed was the jury room. I thought about some serious cases that might have been tried in the same room but couldn't believe that the accused criminals were much more concerned about the juries' verdicts than we were that day.

We just sat and watched the door, not talking much. Even Kirbo seemed uptight. Finally the door opened, and Judge Crow emerged, turned to his right, and walked toward a table that had three chairs behind it, facing us. Sam Singer came next, and we couldn't tell anything from his expression. Then Billy Horne came out, looked over at us with a silly grin, and held up two fingers in a victory sign.

I clutched Rosalynn's hand and tried not to let myself react to Billy's signal. In a few minutes, Judge Crow announced in quiet and emotionless phrases what the panel had decided in a two-to-one vote about the Georgetown box. He read from some notes:

"Upon opening the box of ballots in Georgetown Thursday, we discovered that the list of persons voting and ballot stubs were absent. No explanation was made of what became of the documents and no effort was made to do so. In fact, the poll holders certified that they did not seal the ballot box, nor did they know who did. They did not know how many ballots had been issued or how many voted in said precinct.

"A total of 431 ballots appeared in the box, while sworn testimony indicated that only 333 persons voted. There also was sworn testimony that there were no voting booths and no provision for a secret ballot.

"The ballot box showing to have been stuffed and it

being impossible to separate the illegal from the legal votes, if any, a majority of the committee finds that the Georgetown precinct vote should not be counted."

Judge Crow stated further that there was no evidence to indicate that the three smaller precincts in the county had falsified their records and that voting results that had been reported from the communities of Bumbleton, Union, and Morris should be counted.

This made the tally for the county 43 for Homer Moore and 33 for me. The total vote count in the election was therefore 2,811 to 2,746 in my favor. We had won!

That night, after the recount ruling had gone in our favor, Warren Fortson and I agreed that whenever we drank bourbon in the future it would be the one named after our favorite judge. And, as a matter of fact, we did drink a lot of Old Crow that evening.

☆☆☆☆☆☆☆☆☆☆☆☆☆☆☆☆☆☆☆☆☆☆☆☆☆☆☆☆☆☆

Victory!

...to Victory?

The recount committee report was immediately mailed to George Stewart in Atlanta and to the Quitman County Democratic Executive Committee. Warren told the news reporters that it was now up to the executive secretary of the state Democratic committee to inform the secretary of state of the recount panel's decision so that the ordinaries of the seven counties could delete Homer Moore's name from the already printed ballots and insert mine instead.

This was Friday, and the general election would be the next Tuesday. We didn't have much time to get all the ballots changed. Rosalynn and I decided to get rubber stamps made and have people ready to go to all the counties to help the ordinaries after they received the proper order from Secretary of State Ben Fortson.

That afternoon, Jesse Bowles announced that Homer Moore would appeal the decision of the recount panel, not to the state committee, as we expected, but to the Quitman County Democratic committee chaired by Joe Hurst! As we had suspected, they were relying on that outdated state supreme court ruling which had stated that the local political leaders were the final arbiters in disputes involving authentication of ballots. Now, paradoxically, we were on a collision course but going in two different directions.

✭ ✭ ✭

For several days Charlie Kirbo had been trying to reach George Stewart, the state party's executive secretary, and his patience was wearing thin. Finally, on Saturday afternoon, November 3, Kirbo had had enough. He decided to appeal directly to the new state chairman, J. B. Fuqua, in Augusta.

Kirbo's trip was an adventure. First, he had to borrow fifty dollars to buy a round-trip plane ticket to Augusta, where he found Fuqua at home. The two men were soon down on the floor at his house, going over the records, rulings, and supporting documents. Then Fuqua called Bob Richardson, lawyer for the state party, who advised him not to do anything without the personal approval of Carl Sanders. Kirbo already knew that Sanders was in Washington on a Coca-Cola plane, so he called Coke headquarters in Atlanta for information on the gubernatorial nominee's schedule. Kirbo finally learned when the plane was scheduled to return Sanders to Augusta, where he also lived. Kirbo hurried to what turned out to be the wrong airport, missed the plane, but finally managed to get through on the phone to the Sanders residence, where he was told that the next governor was getting a haircut. Kirbo then took a taxi to the Sanders home and waited for him there. After listening to an explanation of the complicated case and consulting with Fuqua and Richardson, Sanders signed the documents declaring that I was the nominee of the party for the Fourteenth Senatorial District.

Kirbo had acted just in time, for George Busbee and Sam Singer were on a similar errand. When they got Sanders on the phone that evening, they were too late. "Well, I hate to tell y'all," Sanders said, "but I just told Charles Kirbo I was going to name Jimmy Carter as the nominee for the Senate, and have already signed the papers."

Kirbo's day, however, was not over. It was now 8:00 P.M., and we still had to get Secretary of State Ben Fortson to certify my name on the ballot. Kirbo was in Augusta with the party's endorsement, but Fortson was in Atlanta, and there were no more flights scheduled for that evening. Fuqua finally made a call for Kirbo to get a small plane and also made arrangements for the plane's owners to accept the lawyer's personal check. Kirbo then flew to Atlanta and found Fortson before he went to sleep. After a lot of questions the secretary of state signed the certification and sent telegrams to the ordinaries of the seven counties in the senatorial district, directing them to display my name on the general election ballot as the nominee.

In the meantime, Homer Moore's supporters had gone forward with their appeal to the Quitman County Democratic committee, which met that same Saturday. Led, as usual, by Joe Hurst, the committee ordered that the decision of Judge Carl Crow's recount panel be held in abeyance, pending a hearing on Monday afternoon to consider the evidence one more time.

It was now clear that we would have to seek an injunction against the implementation of the local committee's decision. As it turned out, the superior court judge with jurisdiction over this dispute was none other than Tom Marshall, who had enlisted Wingate Dykes, Warren Fortson, and Charles Kirbo in his own disputed election recount two years earlier. We filed our papers with Judge Marshall, and on Sunday afternoon we were informed that he wanted to see us the next day in Leesburg, where he was holding court.

The newspapers weighed in on this latest dispute in their Sunday editions. John Pennington reported in the *Atlanta Journal* that J. B. Fuqua had announced that he was certifying me to Secretary of State Fortson, who had wired all county ordinaries in the Fourteenth District to put my name on the ballot. After reporting Joe Hurst's conflicting announcement, Pennington added, "Thus the political committee responsible for holding the fraudulent election in the first place had at least temporarily overruled an adverse decision against itself." Pennington also quoted Judge Carl Crow as saying, "Under existing election laws, any election can be stolen."

Our case finally made the front page of the *Columbus Ledger* that Sunday morning as well. Under the headline "Moore Plans Write-in Bid," the article quoted Homer's statement about the decision of the recount committee and state Democratic officials in Atlanta. Homer said, "Manipulation by my enemies caused the recount and the subsequent dismissal of the Georgetown box. I carried five of seven counties in the October 16 race and even with the loss of Quitman am still the leader in four of the seven counties." He went on to say that he would be mounting a write-in campaign if his name was taken off the ballot.

After we learned that the secretary of state had directed the seven ordinaries to replace "Homer Moore" with "Jimmy Carter" on all the ballots, Rosalynn, our boys, my sister Gloria, Mother, and some volunteers went to the county seats on Sunday morning to assist the officials in this duty. The ones that could be found were polite and welcomed the help. These ballots were sheets about the size of a card table that included the names of all local and statewide Democratic nominees who had won their elections on September 12. Since there were no Republican candidates in the district, most of the space was taken up by a number of constitutional amendments up for voter consideration. The majority of the ballots were still in the courthouses in the smaller counties, but some had already been sent out to the precinct voting managers. By nighttime, more than half the ballots had been changed, and there would be plenty of time on Monday to complete the job.

Charlie Kirbo drove back to Plains on Sunday morning, still showing the strain from his grueling schedule on Saturday. He brought his five-year-old son, Charles, Jr., with him, fully expecting to drive back to Atlanta that evening, but as it became clear that we had to appear before Judge Marshall the next day, Kirbo once again changed his plans. He, Warren, and I spent most of Sunday afternoon and night together, talking over the issues that we might have to face the next day.

Now, after all the campaigning, voting, and political and legal maneuvering, the case was in the hands of Tom Marshall. His decision would be based on unprecedented and conflicting interrelationships among old legal verdicts, new laws, and party rules, a struggle between state and local political authority, and two contending litigants who were well known to him.

Tom and I were both graduates of the U.S. Naval Academy. After resigning from the navy, Tom had gone to law school and then practiced his new profession in Americus before running for judge. His family was probably the wealthiest in our county, in the banking and wholesale grocery business.

I can't really remember how Rosalynn and I voted in the superior court judge's race in 1960. I do recall, however, that Marshall's opponent, Charlie Burgamy, was a great favorite with our farmer customers because his family was poor and he had been a competent and popular prosecuting attorney. They were both good men, and we may have voted either way. In any case, our family was not particularly involved for one or the other.

That Sunday afternoon, I recalled that Wingate Dykes had made it clear to me that my opponent had been an instrumental supporter of the judge in his narrow victory. However, Charlie Kirbo reassured me that Judge Marshall would not be swayed by personal political obligations. For some reason, Kirbo seemed much more confident than Warren or I about what might happen the next day.

About the only thing we could do was seek an injunction against Joe Hurst and his Quitman County committee to prevent their holding the scheduled hearing that could reverse the decision of the recount committee and interfere with the instructions that had been issued in Atlanta.

Homer Moore's attorneys already had their appeal filed, based on the ruling of Joe Hurst's committee. They asked Judge Marshall to strike both names off the ballot, making the additional claim that it was unconstitutional to throw out the votes in just one precinct within a district and let the other votes be counted.

★★★

On Monday morning, Judge Marshall held a hearing in the Leesburg courthouse, where court was in session. I was not there, being still involved in changing the last of the ballots to include my name. The discussion of our case went on for several hours, broken up every now and then by the judge's other duties. Kirbo still had his small son with him. Joe Hurst, who was the only one there not participating in the legal arguments, volunteered to take care of little Charlie, and they got along well while both of them waited. Joe even took the boy out to lunch.

Judge Marshall restrained the Quitman committee from adversely acting on the recount committee's action, but he raised some serious questions about whether all the votes in the senatorial district should have been recounted. He finally ordered all seven ordinaries to appear at a six o'clock hearing that evening at the Sumter County courthouse to continue arguments in the case. Since this would be just thirteen hours before they would have to conduct elections in their home counties, some of the ordinaries announced that they would not come. Judge Marshall ordered the sheriffs to bring them to Americus.

★ *163*

As the time for the hearing approached, Rosalynn and I felt sure that Judge Marshall would rule according to what he thought was right and fair, which, of course, would uphold our position. However, Charlie Kirbo now went out of his way to let us know that it would be a close call, that it could go either way with legal justification. The question was whether the judge would decide to uphold the decisions from the recount panel and the state officials or just wipe the slate clean and let the voters make a choice all over again. Looking back on it, I think Kirbo had assessed Marshall's questions that morning as an indication that the ruling would go against us.

That Monday night in Americus still seems like an interminable dream. There was not much I could do except to ask the lawyers every now and then what was going on, to reassure Rosalynn and my mother that everything was all right, to wander up and down the courthouse corridors, to pray for a favorable decision from the judge, and to talk to other idle observers about the weather, crop yields, or whatever would pass the time as the big clocks ticked toward midnight.

Judge Marshall spent more time talking to the ordinaries than he did listening to Charlie Kirbo and Homer's lawyers. All the county officials were there except the one from Chattahoochee, where less than a hundred people had voted because most of the county was covered by the Fort Benning military base.

Kirbo decided that our best bet was to stall, since it was likely that Judge Marshall would rule against us and any delay would make it more difficult to change the ballots. The judge was obviously ready to rule, but Kirbo requested a chance to argue our case, saying that it would not take too long. Though Kirbo considered Marshall a good man and a friend, he decided to try the judge's patience by talking at great length. Judge Marshall finally brought the discussion to an end and then announced that all the names should be removed from the ballots and a totally new election held.

In later years, after retiring as chief justice of the Georgia supreme court, Judge Marshall explained his rationale for the ruling: "My main consideration was to let the voters make the decision about who should be their state senator. There was no doubt that the Georgetown ballot box was shot through with fraud, and there was no way to tell how the people in that precinct had wanted to vote. However, there were forty-five other precincts in the district, and none of them had been recounted or challenged. There may have been errors in some of them. No one will ever know. This was what bothered me most, as far as the law was concerned, that all the district's ballots were not recounted. As far as justice was concerned, as I said, why not let the voters start all over with a clean slate and write in the name of their choice?"

The ordinaries, having different priorities from Judge Marshall, argued that it would be almost impossible to change the ballots again in the middle of the night, with voting to begin at seven o'clock the next morning. The judge replied that he knew it would be difficult but certainly not impossible.

Robert Ellis, from Quitman County, was the only one who did not join in this complaint. During the hearing Judge Marshall gave him an opportunity to make a statement, and he said, "Your Honor, I believe that there was a wrong conducted in my county. Everyone up to this point who was in a position to correct that error has not done it. Nobody in authority has done it. It has come down to the point that I might be able to make a decision to do something about it, and whatever I do, I'm going to try to correct the wrong that was done in Quitman County in this election."

When the arguments and counterarguments were finished, long after midnight, Judge Marshall personally served each ordinary with his order to take both names off the ballots. But when he gave the order to Ellis, the Quitman County official looked at him and said, "Your Honor, I have all the respect in the world for the judicial system, and consider myself part of it. I have great respect for you as a judge. But I want you to pray for me, because between here and Georgetown I'm going to decide what to do with this order you've given me."

In later years, Ellis would recall that "it was not an easy decision, because you don't just defy a superior court judge when he personally hands you an order. I hated to defy the court, but I had no reservations but that a wrong had been committed. I honestly felt, and I'm very serious about this, that I thought I could do a little something to show forth that Quitman County was not completely without morals." Ellis also turned down an invitation from Sam Singer to have a drink with him that night, preferring to keep his own counsel about what to do.

Many of the other ordinaries expressed reservations as well. Judge Robert Hawkins, the Sumter County ordinary, told Tom Marshall, "Judge, I have the highest respect for you. My daddy was a lawyer and so am I, and we've known you since you were a boy. But in spite of your ruling, I'm not going to be able to change all the ballots here in the middle of the night. They've already been sent out to the polling places."

Another ordinary, from one of the small counties, said, "Judge Marshall, I heard what you might do before I left home. I knelt down and asked the Lord for guidance, and I haven't heard from Him."

Marshall replied, "No matter if it's the Lord tells you to violate my order, you'll be held in contempt of court."

Warren Fortson overheard Judge Hawkins say to the other ordinaries, "I would rather be in contempt of Judge Marshall than Secretary of State Fortson."

Charlie Kirbo left the courtroom unsatisfied but still feeling that in his own way Tom Marshall had given us a partial victory. "I knew Tom to be a good man, with a lot of pressure on him from Sam Singer and them," he later said, referring to Homer's advocates. "He's never told me, but I kind of felt that he was cooperating with us in a way by letting us drag it out so long that night."

I saw it differently. Judge Marshall's ruling, I felt, was exactly what Homer Moore was asking for, and totally against us. He declared that there were no qualified candidates for the senate seat in the Fourteenth District and issued a restraining order that prevented any ordinary from furnishing voters with any ballot that had my name on it. (By this time we had changed them all.) He announced that all the voting was to be by writing in our names, but this was not included in his official order. I heard one of the ordinaries ask him how many days he would give them in jail, and Marshall replied that he was sure that would not be necessary.

We were angry, but there was nothing else we could do now except vote, try to get our supporters to do the same thing, and make some feeble, last-minute efforts on radio stations to explain the complicated situation and ask for support.

All that day I was so exhausted that I felt like a zombie as I drove around to the different voting places to encourage my supporters. The radio spots were confusing as the situation was explained to listeners from conflicting points of view, about evenly divided between mine and Homer's. I found that my name had been struck from the ballots in all the counties except Sumter and Quitman. This gave me an advantage, but I wasn't worrying about what might be perfectly fair for my opponents, who believed that the recount hearing was unjustified, the decisions of the state Democratic officials were erroneous, and the last-minute striking of my name off all the ballots was the best way to resolve the issue. We never tried to influence any of the ordinaries, and there was no need to argue with their individual decisions. Some of them told me later that they had gone home and called their local attorneys to seek advice on what to do. It seemed that almost all the lawyers had advised them not to be in contempt of the superior court. But then again, they didn't practice law before the secretary of state.

That election night was another difficult one. For some reason, almost all the returns came in before Sumter County's, and Homer Moore was ahead for a while. In fact, having returns from twenty-four of the forty-six precincts in the district, including most of those from Stewart and Terrell counties, the *Atlanta Constitution* went to press with Homer the apparent winner by a close margin. At our warehouse office, we were comparing each county's results with those of the first election, and our percentage had improved in all but one of the six that were reported. I even gained some strength in Homer Moore's county, carrying Lumpkin, Sam Singer's hometown. It was interesting to see the effect on voters of my name being on the ballot. In fact, my vote stayed about the same in Sumter County with the Americus count still not reported, an indication that the rural people had held firmly to their choices from the previous election. However, there was a dramatic change in Quitman County, where voters now free from Joe Hurst's domination and casting secret ballots had reversed their support from the fraudulent count of 360 to 136 for Homer Moore to an overwhelming 448 to 23 in my favor.

We were encouraged, but for several hours it was still too close to call. Then, quite late, the Americus returns, 941 to 148, put me over the top. The final count was 3,013 to 2,182 in my favor. Although two of the ordinaries had not carried out Judge Marshall's order, he had not outlawed the counting of ballots in those counties. Now, while Homer huddled with his lawyers to decide on their next step, Tom Marshall stated that he would take no action against officials in the counties that had failed to delete my name unless charges were brought before him. "I am not an enforcement officer," he said. "Any further action will have to come from one of the parties involved in the suit."

This statement was widely covered in the news,

but the *Columbus Enquirer* added a further disturbing statement not reported anywhere else: "If one or both of the candidates contests the election, then it is very likely that I will rule the election of the 14th Senatorial District invalid."

I went home and collapsed. I was completely out of it for at least twenty-four hours. Except to take one telephone call, I never got out of bed, even to eat. I had lost eleven pounds during the last two weeks.

★ ★ ★

The next day, Homer Moore told some news reporters that he was not going to file an appeal. About nine o'clock that night, he called me and we had a relatively friendly but rambling conversation. When I had hung up the phone, I told Rosalynn that he sounded almost as tired as I was and that he had indicated that it was all over. I was still not sure what he was going to do.

Thursday morning, Homer told the *Atlanta Journal*, "I slept on it last night, and I talked with my lawyer this morning. I decided that I might change my mind."

He said the change of mind could come later that day and that he would take some action on Friday. When asked what action, he replied, "I don't know whether you'd call it a contest or a court order."

I was quoted only as saying, "I've won fairly."

Then, on Saturday morning, the Columbus newspaper editors, after having covered the entire election process in what seemed to us a highly biased fashion, published a column on the editorial page. The first two paragraphs read:

Homer L. Moore of Richland fought the good fight. He fought from spring to fall in this upheaval year for Georgia politics. He won his first race under the old Senate rotation system, beating out a strong field of challengers in his home county.

When the rotation system was abolished, Moore dutifully took his bid to the additional counties that formed the new district with Stewart. One of these included medium-sized Sumter, which furnished his special election opponent Jimmy Carter.

Then came an outline of the recent events, followed by the last two paragraphs:

Mr. Carter's efforts to seek a just verdict in his race are commendable. He will be rewarded with a seat of considerable influence in the renovated state senate. Mr. Moore, as we mentioned, was a symbol of perseverance. He ran for the same office three times in one year, winning twice, but losing the one that finally counted.

But if the Carter-Moore contest results in more conscientious procedures in Georgetown voting, then there will be many winners, including the cause of democracy.

But that afternoon, Homer Moore announced that he would indeed contest the result of the election. Obviously angry, he said, "I'm taking action." When asked what that action would be, he said that he had no other statement to make and that the reporters could consult his lawyers.

Asked to name his attorneys, Homer snapped, "I don't think I'll tell you. You dig that up."

Jesse Bowles then issued a statement saying that Mr. Moore would be announcing his own plan personally, possibly during the next week.

✱✱✱

As promised, a motion was filed in Sumter County on Tuesday, November 13, to have a hearing on the failure of Sumter County Ordinary Hawkins and Quitman County Ordinary Ellis to carry out the order of Judge Marshall. The hearing was scheduled for November 30. Warren and Kirbo consulted by telephone, and Warren told me that they would prepare for an appeal of Judge Marshall's ruling to a higher court if it should become necessary. Now it was strictly a legal matter that only the lawyers and judges could decide. There was nothing else for me to do.

But as this date approached, unusual things started happening. Robert Ellis reported receiving a telephone call instructing him to leave his office and be in court in Americus at a certain time, or else he would be subpoenaed to appear. He described what happened next:

"I left the courthouse, got in my car, and started to drive away. I saw my brother Seab right in front of Duck Graddy's service station, Mrs. Ina's husband. I stopped to talk to Seab, and I saw a state patrol car come around the curve, driving fast. They knew me and knew my car, and I saw the driver swerve over toward us and slam on brakes right by us.

"I said, 'Oh my God, they've got me for contempt of court!'

"I didn't want to go, but knew I had to face the music. The patrolman got out of his car and walked over to me.

"He said, 'Judge, I've got a message for you. You are not to come to court this afternoon, and not until you are officially notified to come.'

"From that day to this, I have never heard from them, and they haven't heard from me. I wanted to know what happened, but didn't want to raise the issue again."

For my part, I received no further statements from Homer Moore or his attorneys until the morning of November 30, when Homer called Warren Fortson to tell him that he had decided not to go through with the hearing. We thought we could finally relax, but, unbeknownst to us, the battle was shifting to another venue.

Homer's lawyers were highly influential with the incoming administration in Atlanta, and they were preparing to take advantage of their position. Jesse Bowles had been a law school classmate of both Tom Marshall and Carl Sanders at the University of Georgia, and they were also fraternity brothers at Chi Phi. Also, George Busbee was well known to be a rising star in the state legislature, a popular and powerful politician. Their plan, which they were careful not to mention publicly, was to take their contest directly to the Senate floor. The law and custom was that the final judgment about any contested seat would be made by the General Assembly itself.

"We were pretty confident about this," Jesse Bowles would later recall. "Busbee was very close to Sanders, and had become very influential in the House of Representatives. We thought that at least Governor Sanders would not play a strong role in a dispute that really involved the

Senate. Peter Zack Geer, who would preside over the Senate and was mighty powerful over there, was a neighbor of mine, and we knew each other well. Most of my law practice was in the Pataula judicial circuit, where his Uncle Walter I. Geer presided."

Although my supporters were breathing a little easier after Homer dropped his court challenge, in reality our position had grown even more tenuous. We had practically no influence at the state capitol. Out of the 259 members of the House and Senate, I knew just a handful who happened to be involved in the certified seed business. By going straight to the Senate, Homer would have all the advantages. He no longer needed to argue his case in public but could appeal directly to the only man who mattered, Lieutenant Governor–elect Peter Zack Geer, a man who owed his election in part to Joe Hurst. As presiding officer of the Senate, Geer could simply refuse to seat me at the opening session and put the case directly before the other elected senators for their final decision. It was not unreasonable to assume that a majority of them would take his advice on how to vote.

chapter 8

✯✯✯✯✯✯✯✯✯✯✯✯✯✯✯✯✯✯✯✯✯✯✯✯✯

Endings
and Beginnings

While Homer Moore and his lawyers were planning to appeal directly to the lieutenant governor and the Senate, I was busy preparing to take my seat in January. We knew that the members of either body of the General Assembly could make the final judgment on who would be seated, but we had no evidence as yet that such a challenge would be made.

One of my main reasons for running for the Georgia Senate had been to improve our region's education system, and I spent much of my time during these weeks thinking about this issue. At the November meeting of our county school board, I told the school superintendent and the other board members that I would be resigning as of January.

We spent a lot of that session talking about some of the things that might be done in Atlanta to improve the situation in Georgia's public schools. And I was still intent on using my new position in the Senate to help establish a four-year college in our part of the state. Our own Georgia Southwestern College in Americus was the best hope for promotion to senior college status, but all the many efforts to accomplish this had been fruitless. My ambition was finally to achieve this goal.

I didn't know much about the inner workings of state government, but I did realize that the governor's greatest influence was in the House; at that time he could even handpick the Speaker. On the other hand, in Georgia the lieutenant governor runs for election on a completely separate platform from the governor and has great authority in the Senate. In addition to presiding over the body in almost all sessions, he determines the composition of the committees. I had never met either Carl Sanders or Peter Zack Geer, who were elected to these two offices in 1962.

Since the entire Senate was now newly constituted as a result of reapportionment, I would be joining a group of freshman legislators, almost all with equal seniority. The few exceptions were those who happened to be completing a two-year term under the old three-county arrangement and had gone on to win a seat in the new districts. By now, all of them (except for me, a handful of Democrats who had been surprised by Republicans, and the still undecided winner in a contested election in Savannah) had known since the October 16 primaries that they had won their elections and would serve. I knew that Lieutenant Governor–elect Geer had been meeting with them for a couple of months, and almost all the preferred committee assignments had been made.

After the legal and political struggles seemed to be over in the Fourteenth District, I went to Atlanta to meet with the Senate's next presiding officer in late November. To me, having been in the state capitol only a few times concerning certified seed or other farm issues, Peter Zack Geer seemed like a potentate presiding over his high council and receiving supplications from his subjects. He was surprisingly young, handsome, with red hair and a red face, and spoke with a deep bass voice. He was known to be highly intelligent, having passed the Georgia bar examination early in his senior year in law school. When his father died immediately thereafter, Peter Zack was given permission to leave college, practice law, and take the final university examinations the following spring. Even under these difficult circumstances, he attained the best academic record of anyone who had ever attended law school at Mercer University.

Above all, perhaps, he was very ambitious and looked on his new job as a stepping-stone to the governor's office four years later. With the reform wave in Georgia resulting from the end of the county unit system, he and other political leaders were naturally eager to moderate their former conservative positions on the race issue and make new friends among a wide range of Georgians, including the newly enfranchised black voters.

It was obvious that he knew all about the Fourteenth District contest, both from the Atlanta newspapers and from his uncle Walter I. Geer, whose judicial circuit included Georgetown. Also, I knew from John Pennington's newspaper articles that Peter Zack had carried Quitman County by a ten-to-one majority during the recent primary, in which the dead, prisoners, and other absent people had cast their votes. Thus, I had helped bring him a lot of publicity that he surely had not wanted.

Peter Zack was friendly and somewhat apologetic as he explained the situation regarding committee assignments and my being so late coming to see him. He then asked me if I had any preferences for the openings still left. I replied that my only request was to be put on the Education Committee, and that I had a special interest in the university system.

He seemed surprised, looked at his committee lists, and said, "Most people want to be on Rules, Appropriations, Judiciary, or Industry and Trade. I haven't had many requests like this, and there's no problem putting you on the Education Committee. However, we don't have anything separate for the colleges."

I told him I was chairman of our school board, ran a farm supply business, and had recently been president of the Georgia Crop Improvement Association. I didn't mention that I had also become an expert on the Georgia election code and Democratic party rules.

He suggested Education and Agriculture, and I agreed.

"If you like to write, keep notes, and so forth, I can make you secretary of the Education Committee," he said. "The higher positions are already promised."

I decided to push my luck and asked if it was possible to form a subcommittee on higher education. He replied that this might be done, but he would have to check with the new head of the committee. He turned around and made a phone call, then said it was okay and that I would be chairman of the Subcommittee on Higher Education. It sounded like an exalted title.

Before leaving his office, I asked about the contest in Savannah, which was between the Republican and Democratic nominees. Peter Zack said he didn't know how it would turn out but added that the final decision would be made by the Senate and not by the political parties or the courts. He watched me closely and with a half smile as he added that some people had already mentioned the possibility of more than one contest, but he hadn't heard much about it. This sent chills down my spine.

Sure enough, as the time approached for convening the legislature, Homer Moore made some comments to his hometown newspaper indicating that he might consider a contest in the Senate when it convened. By that time our election was old news, and this item was not covered anywhere else. I saw Homer at a meeting of peanut warehousemen in Albany, and we met to shake hands. After we talked about things such as peanut storage rates, warehouse inspections, grading standards, and insecticides that could be used, he brought up the election.

"Some of my folks in Stewart County are still asking me not to give up," he said, "but I think I'll be better off staying at home and getting some of your best customers while you're up in Atlanta."

Charlie Kirbo thought the best thing for us to do was to lie low and not raise the issue publicly or start campaigning among the newly elected senators. We would just monitor the situation and hope that the Senate would not want to be involved in two contests simultaneously. It could be that Homer would find this effort so formidable that he would give up the idea. Although he had not been involved in any fraudulent acts himself, there had been a lot of state-wide publicity about our case, and the names of Homer Moore and Joe Hurst were closely linked in people's minds.

★ ★ ★

In January, as the time approached for all the legislators to assemble in Atlanta for the opening session of the General Assembly, neither our lawyers nor I knew what to expect. It was up to Peter Zack Geer. He could just direct that I not be sworn in, that a special committee be formed to consider the contest in our district, and that a final decision be made later. We could then go to court or try to prevail in the Senate, but this struggle might continue past the end of the session, which under the Georgia constitution was limited to forty-five working days. When Rosalynn and I drove to Atlanta for the 1963 General Assembly session, we wondered whether this contest would be over in time for me to serve any part of my term. The suspense was a constant burden.

It had long been the custom of Georgia legislators to have a party the night before the legislative session, with plenty of whiskey flowing and the main course for supper being barbecued wild hog. The Henry Grady Hotel was the site of this event. The hotel lobby and all the corridors would be packed, with the governor, lieutenant governor, Speaker of the House, and the cabinet officers taking this opportunity to meet the new legislators and then to meet one another.

Rosalynn and I were there, somewhat timid because of our newness and uncertain status. As we pushed our way toward Peter Zack's suite so that Rosalynn could meet him, we saw Homer Moore, Sam Singer, and Jesse Bowles coming out. We nodded to each other as we passed. Sam and Homer had broad grins on their faces, which made us more nervous than ever, if that was possible, about what was going to happen when the Senate convened the next day.

✳ ✳ ✳

Early the next morning I walked from the hotel to the state capitol and went into the Senate chamber. It was empty except for one man, who introduced himself as Joe Tribble, from Savannah. He was the Republican candidate who was facing the contest for the Third District seat. He knew who I was when I mentioned my name and asked if I was in the same boat.

"I hope not," I said, "but I'm not sure."

A couple of hours later, when Peter Zack finally gaveled the Senate to order, the first item of business was to swear in the members. He announced that we should come forward ten at a time, gather around the clerk, raise our right hands, and take the oath. Then he called out, "Will the senators-elect from Districts One through Ten come forward, except for the Third. I have been informed that there is a contest pending in that district."

Nine new senators took their oath, while Tribble and his opponent stayed in their back seats.

I watched the first group of senators taking the oath of office, still not sure what would come next. I feared hearing the words "except for the Fourteenth District." As he started to call the next group, Peter Zack looked at me and hesitated. I glanced up at Rosalynn, sitting on the edge of her seat in the balcony. She had her eyes closed. Then he said, "Will the senators-elect from Districts Eleven through Twenty come forward." That's all he said. I moved forward and raised my hand. A few seconds later I was a state senator.

✶✶✶✶✶✶✶✶✶✶✶✶✶✶✶✶✶✶✶✶✶✶✶✶✶✶✶✶✶✶

What Did It
All Mean?

Mr. President, I move that the proposed Georgia election code be amended as follows: 'No person may vote either in the Democratic primary or in the general election in the State of Georgia who has been deceased more than three years.' "

It was February 1964, in the Georgia Senate. The amendment was offered by Senator Bobby Rowan from Enigma, a town in south Georgia even smaller than Georgetown or Plains. There followed a lively debate concerning the exact time interval between death and the loss of voting privileges. We assessed how long the spirit and political orientation of dead citizens might still be remembered, applied to current circumstances, and expressed with fair accuracy by survivors as the likely choice of the deceased if they had lived until election day. Although this exchange was humorous, the events leading up to it had been serious indeed.

As was long overdue, the many carefully nurtured loopholes in the Georgia election code, which had kept men like Joe Hurst in power, were now being closed, to the discomfort of some of the statehouse politicians. Many of them owed their high positions to the corrupt and unfair but legal practices that had long been integral facets of our state's election scene.

The year 1962 was a turning point, in that the tides of political history were changed. The combination of white Democratic primaries and rural bias in voting and apportionment that had for generations held the South in thrall were now to be just a fading memory.

Today, three decades after the death of the county unit system, many things are different in Quitman County, the Fourteenth Senatorial District, Georgia, and the South. Georgia political campaigns and elections have, almost invariably, become both open and honest. The votes of urban dwellers have approximately equal weight with those of farmers and residents of small towns. Former Democrats and their children have been able to switch to the Republican party without disappearing into the abyss of political obscurity. For better or worse, there is a strong two-party political system in the state.

The Civil Rights Act of 1964 has slowly been implemented by civil rights workers, federal agents, and state officials liberated from the burden of official racism. Federal judges and other Justice Department officials still monitor election procedures in our region and oversee every reapportionment of congressional and state legislative districts to assure proper racial balance. Black citizens have legal rights to use public facilities, to eat alongside white customers where meals are served to the public, to participate in electing public officials, and to run for office themselves. In many sports and in entertainment, black Americans are ascendant, as they are in the governing bodies of many of our major cities. State legislatures and the U.S. Congress are slowly but inexorably becoming more racially balanced. It seems that the original goals of the civil rights movement have been attained.

However, social and economic barriers to racial equality and better lives are still prevalent. In some ways our society has improved very little since 1962. Political analysts differ on whether the newly empowered urban legislators in the South are significantly more progressive on most issues than were their more rural predecessors. As a state senator and governor, I found that on many subjects the more representative legislature was little changed.

But there is no doubt that there has been significant improvement on the race issue. Just having one forceful black person in any kind of forum has a profound impact. Even without a verbal exchange, white leaders are more likely to accommodate minority sensitivities and needs if a member of that group is present. There was a quick learning process in the state Senate when Leroy Johnson took his seat following the 1962 election. We, his fellow senators, did not know whether to say "colored," "black," or "Negro" in referring to him and his race. South Georgians, in particular, had difficulty in pronouncing the word of his choice, having it come out something like "ni-grur." Patiently, Senator Johnson pointed to his knee, and then made a rising motion with his right hand. We practiced a few times, until finally he nodded his approval. From then on, we carefully enunciated "Knee-grow."

Leroy Johnson quickly became a valued ally for his white colleagues. Many faced for the first time the need to campaign among newly enfranchised black constituents. Senator Johnson was generous with his time and advice, and would visit districts throughout Georgia to assist legislators who earned his confidence. He used this influence with great advantage to black Georgians.

Unfortunately, social and economic factors have counterbalanced the painfully gained legal rights in many ways. With the demise of the county unit system, both rural white citizens and their black neighbors lost political power. Would-be governors, members of Congress, and state legislators changed their campaign strategies to accommodate the shift toward urban power, for they could no longer depend on the rural counties to deliver enough votes to elect them. Folks in the country are consequently not wooed as they used to be, and many of the old personal political relationships are gone. Candidates now realized that their effort is best spent where large numbers of supporters can be sought most efficiently, with the least cost in time and money per vote. Large and expensive appearances in rural county seats, with free barbecues and country music, have become part of history. Not nearly as many hands are shaken or friendships made. Increasingly, slick and impersonal television spots have become the foundation of campaigns, with a few ostentatious visits to small towns thrown in as bucolic media events.

State officials are no longer as willing to concentrate government services such as roads, schools, and job opportunities in the small counties. More important, the end of county bossism has resulted in a more impersonal and less caring relationship between local officials and their constituents. In the old days, everyone knew where to go with a problem, and the local boss had direct access to state officials, who had to be sensitive to his requests in order to get the unit votes he could deliver. Now, it is more difficult to understand the political chain of command or follow it to a favorable decision.

There is little doubt, for instance, that Joe Hurst and his wife, Mary, knew every black and white citizen in Quitman County, having personally delivered monthly welfare checks to the poor families—about half the total population. Whatever criticisms his fellow citizens might level at him, they all acknowledge that "Joe took care of his people." These favors were available even to those who had worked and voted against the Hurst candidates on election day. For those political foes who were willing to request his help, there was at least an implied promise of accommodation in the future. This degree of personal politics rarely exists today, having been replaced for poorer people by encounters with a faceless postal service and a constantly changing cadre of social workers with whom there is little real empathy.

But it is the education system in the South that has borne the brunt of social change. When the public schools were first required to integrate in the wake of *Brown v. Board of Education*, there was a mass exodus of white students whose parents could pay the tuition fees to enroll in the private "segregation academies" that sprang up in almost all communities. A few of these private schools have flourished and developed good academic programs, but most have not been able to compete in terms of quality and have based their continuing existence on parental dedication to racial segregation. Even worse, many public school boards have come to be dominated by affluent members whose children attend the community's private schools. Inevitably, their interests tend to be concentrated more on holding down the property tax rates that finance the public schools than on providing adequate support to enhance the curriculum in the schools their children do not attend.

In the meantime, though, the integrated high school athletic teams have brought black and white fans together in football and basketball stadiums and have made it easier for them to accept biracial classrooms. Over the years, dwindling enrollments in the weaker private academies have caused them to close, and their students have been returning to the public system, at least in the rural communities. In large cities, however, where housing patterns are based on family income, many of the schools are once again almost totally segregated. It is obvious that neither the promised blessings nor the dire predictions of school integration have been realized.

Even under the best circumstances, the degree to which integration is accepted in the schools can be misleading. After spending ten years in public schools, our daughter, Amy, chose to attend a large private boarding school near Atlanta to get advanced college preparatory and art courses. Although fairly expensive and attended mostly by white students, the school had completely integrated programs, with all classes and extracurricular events encouraged to be biracial. The students seemed to be almost totally color-blind. When Rosalynn and I asked Amy how many of her fellow students were black, it was obvious that she had never thought about them in that way. One of her friends was James Forman, Jr., son of the first executive director of the Student Nonviolent Coordinating Committee. When Amy told us that she, James, and other black and white teenagers were going to the graduation dance together, it seemed natural. However, in a few days she called home, angry and distressed. The school officials had informed the student body that no "mixed" couples would be admitted. A social event was different from the campus or the classroom. When she asked us what to do, we encouraged her to use her own judgment. Not surprisingly, she and James informed the school superintendent that they would violate the ruling and go together. They did so and were not stopped at the door. This was in 1985.

Religious congregations also reflect society's ambivalence toward integration. A few formerly segregated Southern churches have been fully integrated, welcoming black members and making them feel that they are brothers and sisters of the white worshipers, but these are the notable exceptions. Even when white church doors are open, differences between black and white congregations in the conduct of religious services form barriers to integration. Our own Maranatha Baptist Church in Plains was formed in 1978 (while we were in Washington) by moderate members who left our mother church, in part because they were willing to have interracial worship. Our congregation exchanges visits on occasion with the black members of Lebanon Baptist Church in Plains, our pastors and choirs share the services, and we welcome black visitors and full-time members. However, of the few nonwhites who have responded to this open invitation, most are from families who have moved into our community from foreign countries. In general, racial segregation is still the norm in Southern churches, which in some communities seems to be what most black and white worshipers prefer.

The 1960s were a time of great hope and expectations. Those of us involved in opening up the political system saw the end of antidemocratic boss rule as the first step in the effort to make our nation live up to its ideals. The "one man, one vote" decision was followed by the Civil Rights Act of 1964, the Voting Rights Act of 1965, and the equal opportunity programs of the Great Society. We did not realize at the time, however, that solving one set of problems does not end all difficulties but, rather, changes their shape. New, unanticipated problems have arisen as the barriers to political participation have fallen—lack of economic progress, insufficient housing, substandard education, and unemployment among our poorest citizens. For two decades, all three branches of the federal government led a steady effort to alleviate these burdens, which fall disproportionately on minorities. However, in the 1980s our national leaders abandoned this commitment, and the ravages of segregation and discrimination (which most of us thought were relics of the past) have once again become prevalent. Our country is growing increasingly polarized along economic lines, and minority citizens suffer most.

When I first ran for the Georgia Senate, there were many black families who owned their own farms and the implements needed to produce a crop. Dozens of them purchased fertilizer, seeds, insecticides, and livestock feed from Carter's Warehouse and brought their cotton to our gin and their peanuts to our storage warehouses. Our competitor across the street had a similar number of these good customers. Now, farms are much bigger and require large investments in sophisticated equipment to make a crop. Federal government policies favoring corporate agriculture, intense economic competition, and the subtle discrimination of banks and other financial institutions have forced black families out of small farm ownership. The warehouse operators in Plains can now name only one active black farmer and landowner left in our community, and this family actually earns a living by manufacturing burial vaults. The interracial sharing of agricultural husbandry and entrepreneurship is rapidly disappearing. A recent study has revealed that rural blacks are losing ownership of about 2,000 acres of Southern farmland every day.

Without farms of their own or the financial ability to work rented land, few of these families can find jobs near their rural homes. Forced to move to urban communities, they are ill equipped for this completely new kind of life. For them and their neighbors, city living can be difficult, and it is growing worse. There is a lack of hope among needy families that their most serious problems will be solved. This hopelessness is often shared by community leaders who have the authority and responsibility for correcting the city's ills. It is easier for city officials and Chamber of Commerce boosters to ignore or deny these problems than to acknowledge and address them forthrightly.

As the social and economic plight of our minority citizens has become more apparent and disturbing, the race issue has crept back into American politics. Even if there is no more talk of a white Democratic primary and few references to the threat of "bloc voting," the political treasure trove of racism is still tapped by some candidates. This was a factor in the 1964 presidential race. Although Barry Goldwater avoided this ploy himself, his campaign managers in the Southern states were less reticent. They understood the subtle euphemisms; one of their most popular bumper stickers read, "I'm against welfare. I work." Goldwater's opposition to Lyndon Johnson's civil rights bills was parlayed into the first victory in history for a Republican presidential candidate in Georgia, a triumph shared only in Alabama, Mississippi, South Carolina, Louisiana, and Goldwater's home state of Arizona.

Playing the race card seems to be a tactic that still wins political contests. It was not a coincidence that Ronald Reagan made his opening "I believe in states' rights" speech of the 1980 presidential campaign in Philadelphia, Mississippi. This was the place where law enforcement officers had murdered three young civil rights workers in 1964 to deter others who were promoting racial integration—the most highly publicized crime of the civil rights era. The 6,200 residents of that town and everyone else involved on both sides of the civil rights movement knew that "states' rights" meant segregation. Subsequently, frequent references from the White House to "welfare queens," public insinuations that Martin Luther King, Jr., was a communist, and a pattern of intercessions by the U.S. attorney general *against* plaintiffs in cases of civil rights abuse were designed to appeal to right-wing constituencies. Likewise, the infamous Willie Horton television spots, with heavy-handed racial overtones, were instrumental in the Republican presidential victory of 1988.

So, what are the overall consequences of the civil rights and electoral reforms of the 1960s? There is no way to know what Southern life would be like now if legal segregation and elections based on rural white supremacy had been perpetuated, but it is beyond question that the new freedoms and equality of opportunity are precious treasures for those who have gained them. Within the reformed legal and political system, there are more opportunities for correcting our social ills; the voices of deprived people can no longer be so easily stilled or their plight ignored. Despite general awareness of these unmet challenges, the tragic fact is that the South and the nation have not succeeded in building a society of justice and equal opportunity on the momentous legal decisions that brought an end to overt racial discrimination.

There is an enormous chasm between the relatively rich and powerful people who make decisions in government, business, and finance and our poorer neighbors who must depend on these decisions to alleviate the problems caused by their lack of power and influence. Even leaders with the best of intentions seldom know personally the families in their communities whose lives are blighted by substandard housing, high crime rates, inferior schools, scarce social amenities, high unemployment, and exorbitant prices in the few nearby stores. In these neighborhoods the average family income is most often less than half the official poverty level. Many students drop out of school, health care and other services are remote or nonexistent, the teenage pregnancy rate is growing, a high percentage of babies are born prematurely and underweight, and the drug culture flourishes. More than 40 percent of America's black babies are born in poverty, often to young mothers who have received little or no prenatal care. Despite some slow progress in reducing the national infant mortality rate, a newborn baby is no more likely to survive in Harlem than in Bangladesh.

The multiplicity of government programs are uncoordinated and poorly designed, administered by top officials who rarely see at first hand why their efforts are so inadequate. Although there are many religious and other benevolent organizations whose workers minister to the poor and attempt to alleviate their problems, these efforts are often confined to one issue or to a very small group of needy families. Little if any overall progress is being made. In fact, conditions in the inner cities are growing worse. In some urban communities, the number of homeless people has increased tenfold in the last decade. The soaring crime rate among our young people is another disturbing indication of this trend. In the five years from 1986 to 1991, offenses involving violence increased 300 percent in the juvenile courts in Atlanta, while crimes involving drugs jumped 1,700 percent!

Our country's history tends to move in cycles, and today we have come to another turning point, as the segregation of our society has become almost as insidious as it was thirty years ago. The division is between rich and poor, but still largely along racial lines. There are now two Atlantas, two Washingtons, two New Yorks, two Detroits, two Americas. Those of us who live in the affluent and comfortable America have homes, jobs, education, health care, and convenient services, while many of our neighbors down the road don't have these things.

The Los Angeles riots in the spring of 1992 revealed the extent of despair and anger implicit in our divided nation, a disturbing state of affairs that Rosalynn and I had already begun to address in our work at the Carter Center. We saw that many families in America's inner cities need attention, as did our black neighbors in south Georgia thirty years ago. Our response has been to help launch a massive effort in Atlanta to address the whole gamut of problems in our most troubled neighborhoods, to coordinate existing private and government services into closer teamwork, and to give needy citizens maximum control over the entire effort. We hope that the successful elements of our Atlanta experience will provide a helpful model for other communities.

Through the Atlanta Project we have targeted the poorest neighborhoods in our own metropolitan area, home to more than 15 percent of our population—about 500,000 people—most of them black or Hispanic. Many of these people, living in areas riddled by crime and the drug culture, have a sense of hopelessness about their future. They don't think the police or the judicial system is on their side, and they don't believe that any decision they make will have an effect, even on their own lives. Tragically, the poor families in our cities are not the only ones who feel that the situation in this country is hopeless. There is an equally troubling belief in the White House, Congress, governors' mansions, city halls, and universities that the best plans and programs cannot make things better.

I do not think the situation is hopeless. We must remember the crises and solutions of the past, build on the achievements, and apply these lessons once again to heal our segregated nation. This is the turning point that we have now reached in the development of our society, when troubled citizens—black and white, poor and rich, liberal and conservative—must seek and find unprecedented ways to work together in solving the challenges of homelessness, unemployment, crime, drugs, and poor education and health care.

Having been caught up in a series of dramatic events, all the way from the Georgetown courthouse to the White House and beyond, I have a sense of the panoramic changes that have occurred since the "one man, one vote" decision was handed down. I am grateful that the millstone of official racism has been removed from the necks of Southerners, both black and white. These reforms have elevated the Southland into equal status with other states for the first time in more than a century. Had this not happened, I could never have been considered as a serious candidate for national office. Overwhelming support from my black neighbors, including the family of Martin Luther King, Jr., helped to alleviate the concerns of voters in other regions about the prospect of electing a Georgia governor to the nation's highest office. I thus became the first president elected from the Deep South in 128 years, since General Zachary Taylor, who made his home in Baton Rouge, Louisiana, won his victory in 1848.

During and since my presidency, I have observed how just laws and democratic procedures in America can offer an end to racial discrimination and human suffering. I have also seen how honest and fair elections in other countries can help end wars and promote democracy. In recent years I have participated personally in helping to arrange and monitor a number of free elections in Latin America and in Africa. I have learned over these years that legal changes and government policies alone are not sufficient to achieve the related goals of justice and freedom. Deprived citizens must help to shape their own destiny. Without a genuine sharing of authority and power, of concerns and fears, of hopes and dreams, little can be done to alleviate human suffering. This unrealized progress remains our challenge for the future.

✷ ✷ ✷

The events of 1962 changed my life and transformed the society in which I live. It may be interesting to note what happened to the other participants in the Georgetown Senate case.

Tom Marshall, the superior court judge who ruled against me the night before the general election, was later elected to the Georgia Court of Appeals, then to the state supreme court, where he became chief justice.

Warren Fortson continued his advocacy of civil rights in the 1960s. But when he and a few other moderate leaders endorsed steps such as the formation of a biracial council to alleviate or prevent confrontations between black and white citizens in Americus, they were forced to leave town. Warren, however, still has a successful law practice and has been attorney for the Atlanta school board for the past twenty years.

Griffin Bell, a member of both federal judicial panels that made the historic reapportionment rulings in 1962 and who suggested that Charles Kirbo might be willing to assist Warren Fortson as my lawyer, served as U.S. attorney general and later managed King and Spalding, one of our nation's largest legal firms.

Charles Kirbo became chairman of the Georgia Democratic party but declined to take any governmental post. Despite this, he has been my most valued and effective adviser, while I served as governor and president, and in private life.

John Pennington was city editor of the *Atlanta Journal* for a while but didn't like the desk job and soon went back to seeking news and writing incisive essays. After living in relative seclusion for several years on Georgia's Cumberland Island, he worked for a short time in Washington and then wrote for the Sunday magazine of the *St. Petersburg Times*. I heard he was terminally ill with cancer in 1980 and went by for a last visit with him. He seemed to be in good spirits, wishing that he could ride back to Washington with me in the cockpit of Air Force One "as payment for helping you get to be president." He died a few weeks later.

Carl Sanders served his four-year term as governor, waited the required four-year interval, then ran for the office again in 1970. I defeated him in a runoff election.

My successor in the governor's office was George Busbee, one of the two attorneys who represented my opponent. Homer Moore's other lawyer, Jesse Bowles, later became a justice of the Georgia Supreme Court.

David Gambrell, the young lawyer who assisted Charles Kirbo in the preparation of legal briefs in my Senate contest, served Georgia in the U.S. Senate after the death of Richard B. Russell.

Homer Moore and Sam Singer continued their careers as successful warehousemen and merchants. They were friendly competitors of mine until I gave up my commercial life to go to the White House. In fact, both Sam and Homer went to New Hampshire as volunteers in my 1976 presidential campaign. Sam was elected to several more terms in the state House of Representatives before retiring voluntarily to private life in Lumpkin. Homer never ran again for the Senate. After I completed two terms in the state Senate and decided to run for governor, my first cousin Hugh Carter was elected to the same seat and served until his retirement fourteen years later.

John Pope, still among our closest personal friends, made some wise initial investments in an insurance company that became an international success, and later helped to form a bank in Sumter County. He and his wife, Betty, my cousin, are among our area's most generous philanthropists.

Peter Zack Geer served a successful term as lieutenant governor but was not able to gain another political office. He has a lucrative law practice in southwest Georgia.

The most involved story is what happened to Joe Hurst. Shortly after the 1962 election, Joe was indicted and later convicted on two felony charges in federal court. One of them was for production and marketing of moonshine whiskey in Quitman County.

Federal agents came to his house one night and asked him if he "had any stuff." Joe put on his shirt and took them out in the woods to meet a local moonshiner who was running the sheriff's still. During the ride, the federal agents stated that they were prepared to pay Doc Hammond fifty cents a gallon extra for protection. Joe replied, into their concealed tape recorder. "Doc Hammond can't protect anything. I'm the one can give you full protection as long as only the sheriff and I know about it." It was this recording that finally sent him to prison. It was clear that, in the state courts, he had a lot of influence and could almost guarantee protection for himself and others. But this was a federal case.

There is real doubt that Joe Hurst was trafficking in moonshine whiskey, at least for his own profit. Even some of his critics think he was just trying to line up customers for his friends and political allies. Doc Hammond should know what was going on, and he still maintains, "Joe was not guilty on the liquor charge. He didn't make a dime on liquor, just told people sometimes where they could get it. That's just the way he was."

I asked Sam Singer about this recently, and he said, "Joe Hurst was a big Mason, and Masons are not in the liquor business. Let's put it this way, Joe supported and protected his friends who made moonshine whiskey."

Along with Hurst, Doc Hammond, the sheriff, and a man who ran the sheriff's moonshine still were also convicted. There were two sting operations, the first one involving Doc Hammond. Twenty-five years later, he still maintained he was not guilty—at least when they caught him.

Laughing, he described what happened:

"I was innocent on the moonshine case, and shouldn't have been convicted. I'd been quit making it five weeks before they picked me up. It was funny. The sheriff was making just fifty gallons a week, and I had been making five hundred. Without knowing it, I carried a federal man out there to show him where to buy some liquor, and since

I hadn't made any in five weeks, I decided to buy me five gallons. I put it in back of my station wagon, in a crocus sack. You couldn't see it.

"Later, in court they asked me and I denied buying it. Then they come out with these pictures of me, plain as everything, standing there with the liquor in my hand. It was one of my best pictures. The agent took it, the pimp I was trying to help."

The other charge was brought against Joe Hurst and five of his associates for election fraud in the September 12 statewide primary, just before our state Senate race. It was a federal case because a congressman and a U.S. senator were being elected, and the charges were based on evidence that had been produced by John Pennington and publicized in his articles about our election dispute. Early in my second year as a state senator, they were all convicted and sentenced to a fine plus probation for three years. Apparently, this had little effect on the Quitman County political escapades. On February 29, 1964, the same day the sentences were announced, the *Columbus Enquirer* ran this article:

> The Quitman County Democratic Executive Committee Friday night refused to qualify Ralph Balkcom, former County School Superintendent, as a candidate for State Representative in the April 2 Democratic Primary. The refusal leaves incumbent Representative Joe Hurst unopposed in his bid for reelection.
>
> Balkcom first was refused qualification on Thursday night by Fane Dykes, committee chairman, on the grounds that the qualification deadline for state offices already had passed.

Ralph Balkcom explained it this way:

"On Monday, Joe Hurst paid in to run for reelection, but they kept it a secret. I found out about it on Wednesday and went down to sign up, but Fane said it was too late. I tried again the next day, and he wouldn't take my money. I remembered John Pennington with the *Atlanta Journal*, who had covered Jimmy's election in 1962. I got Jimmy to call him, and he came back to Georgetown to cover my trouble. Jimmy also came over, and we three walked over to Fane's house. Pennington took a picture of me handing Fane the money, but he still wouldn't take it. It was a big story."

The state committee directed the county committee to reschedule the election in July, which gave Ralph time to qualify as a candidate. By then, Joe Hurst had had to resign from his state job and the legislature because his final felony conviction had come through, so his wife, Mary, ran in his place. That was the hottest race ever in the county. All night the vote count seesawed back and forth between Hurst and Balkcom. Ralph finally won by twenty-five votes.

Later, as a state senator, I went over to the House chamber to hear Ralph make his first and last speech in the legislature. The other members listened closely as he described a passing era.

He said, "I'm from one of the two smallest counties in the state, maybe the smallest by now. We're going to reapportion this session, and Quitman County will never again have its own representative. Pine trees are replacing our folks, and a few people have been controlling things. I know I won't be back next year, and some laws need to be changed. These local bills are our last chance to have honest elections." His election reform bills for his county passed, and I saw to it that they got through the Senate in a hurry.

On an October 1991 visit to Quitman County, I talked to Robert Ellis, the ordinary who had refused to remove my name from the ballot on general election day in 1962. He had heard that I was in Georgetown and came to the courthouse to find me.

He reminisced, "I've retired now because of a weak heart, but I still come to the ordinary's office every day. That 1962 election is a vivid memory for me. I think back on those few days with a feeling that I was involved in a small way in making history. Just think, there I was in the judge's office in Americus the night before the general election, in the room with two men who would be governors, two supreme court justices, a lawyer working with a young man who would be a U.S. senator, and a future president. And there I was, not knowing or caring much what would happen in Georgia or the nation, but just what might take place in Quitman County the next day and maybe in later elections. Looking back on it all, it's a sobering thought."

It is obvious to anyone driving through on Georgia Route 27 that Georgetown mirrors the changing character of most rural villages during the last three decades. The downtown stores are closed, put out of business by quick-service car stops along the highways approaching the main street. They provide gasoline, ready-made sandwiches, minnows and worms for fishing, and a small stock of groceries at exorbitant prices relative to those of city supermarkets. For each purchase, customers must compare the higher price with the cost and inconvenience of driving across the river to Eufaula and back.

There are not nearly as many state jobs in Quitman County as there were when it had its extraordinary voting and legislative power under the county unit system. Joe Hurst served his term in federal prison, died in Alabama in 1973, and was buried in Georgetown. The people are free now to cast their votes (greatly deflated to equal in value those in Atlanta) in honest elections, a freedom that has erased much of the drama, tension, and excitement from Georgia politics.

Now, so long after the fateful 1962 election, I can see the events with much more humor and less personal bias. It was a turning point for me, and a harbinger of almost revolutionary changes in politics, government, and a way of life. Since these things happened, Georgetown and Quitman County have not been the same.

And neither have I.

Appendix

✳✳✳✳✳✳✳✳✳✳✳✳✳✳✳✳✳✳✳✳✳✳✳✳✳✳✳

The Atlanta
Project

The events of the 1962 campaign opened my eyes not only to the ways in which democratic processes can be subverted, but also to the capacity of men and women of good will to engage the system to right such wrongs. Throughout my career in public service I have sought to meet this challenge. It is in this spirit that Rosalynn and I are spearheading the effort we call the Atlanta Project.

The greatest domestic challenge of our nation is to improve the quality of life in America's inner cities. Despite a vast array of government and private programs designed to find solutions, the multiple problems associated with poverty are growing in severity. There is a sense of hopelessness among poor families who do not believe that their lives will ever improve, and an equally serious lack of hope among political and other leaders who doubt that any amount of additional funds or personnel will make a difference. Only an extraordinary initiative is likely to overcome this common sense of despair and generate a chance of success.

The Atlanta Project is a community effort of unprecedented range and complexity. Approximately 500,000 people live in our targeted area, more than 15 percent of the population of the metropolitan area. This is roughly half the disadvantaged families in the state of Georgia. Although there are varying degrees of need, many families suffer from several of the ills The Atlanta Project is preparing to address: poverty, homelessness, unemployment, teen pregnancy, lack of health care, inability to complete high school, and life in neighborhoods of crime and drug sales. Less than one-third of the families are headed by married couples, and a high proportion are on welfare, live in substandard housing, and suffer from chronic unemployment. Understandably, such troubling statistics generate concern and skepticism that anything can succeed.

Many organizations of benevolent and dedicated professionals and volunteers are already attempting to alleviate the suffering of our unfortunate neighbors, some with notable success. In addition to concern for the poor, another motivation for action is the realization that burgeoning inner city problems endanger the quality of life of everyone in the city and suburbs. More and more, juvenile crime and the drug culture reach out to touch all young people. Uneducated citizens are potentially valuable but wasted community resources and provide employers with poorly qualified workers. Unsafe streets and blighted neighborhoods are a shared embarrassment. Incarceration of increasing numbers of prisoners (about $35,000 annually for each) and medical care for indigent mothers and their premature and underweight babies (sometimes as much as $300,000 per child) are enormous costs to taxpayers that may be substantially reduced. All too often, our universities are teaching in a vacuum about the vital characteristics of human existence. Professors and students in such subjects as sociology, anthropology, public health, law, religion, or political science rarely have any direct involvement in the valuable case studies that are on the college doorsteps. It is obvious that the total community can benefit from a sharing of responsibilities and opportunities.

It is doubtful if adequate resources of a metropolitan community can be marshaled if only one or two problems are addressed at a time, and within relatively small geographical areas. The Atlanta Project has aroused a high level of interest and support because it *is* grand in scope, idealistic, challenging, adventurous, and potentially gratifying.

✷ ✷ ✷

As we have explored the situation in Atlanta more deeply, some principles and guidelines have become clear.

I. A "Santa Claus" or charity approach will simply not work. Even the accepted practice of providing a stream of new or improved services to needy families will, at best, give only transient benefits. Soup kitchens, homeless shelters, food stamps, housing assistance, schools in juvenile detention centers, and emergency health care are all valuable but give little promise of permanent change in living conditions.

Our goal must be to develop lasting improvements in the lives of our disadvantaged neighbors, working side by side with them as partners so they can demonstrate their ambition, dependability, and competence. As much as possible, they should be encouraged to play the dominant role in these partnerships, and so gain new levels of self-reliance and control over their own neighborhoods. This will, by the way, mean the relinquishing of some power by those leaders who now make the decisions. As we have already experienced, people in the cluster communities are not reticent about asserting their views or demanding the right to shape their own future. This is a good foundation on which to build.

II. One of the vital roles The Atlanta Project has to play is to improve understanding between current civic leaders and families that are afflicted with poverty. We must provide a practical plan for community progress that will inspire people to work together to reach bold and exciting goals. We must strive to eliminate the legal and bureaucratic obstacles that have prevented solutions of problems in the past. We must recruit a vast array of volunteer persons and organizations and assign them tasks so specific that there will be no doubt about individual responsibilities to make The Atlanta Project successful.

III. The several hundred federal, state, and local government agencies and private organizations that are dealing with the problems of crime, poor housing, inadequate health care, and unemployment do not comprise a team. In most cases they operate with independent management and authority, rarely find opportunities to cooperate with each other, and lack either the motivation or neutral arena within which they can organize a common effort. There is no comprehensive plan or design within which the enormous available resources can be focused in harmony for maximum effectiveness. The Atlanta Project will attempt to overcome this handicap, with careful planning and with strong and concerted collaboration among these existing programs. Advice will be sought routinely from educational, religious, governmental, and business leaders, and from those who manage existing benevolent organizations. We will offer them full support and will not duplicate these good efforts. We will seek legal authorization at all levels of government to cut through red tape, to simplify and consolidate forms, and to encourage maximum coordination of different agencies.

IV. From the perspective of needy families struggling to buy food, obtain medical care, or pay rent, there is an almost impenetrable morass of application forms, multiple and distant agencies, confusing regulations, and fragmented responsibilities. To them it seems that most decisions are made in Washington, the state capitol, city halls, school boardrooms, or health offices with little input from the people most personally affected. Promises of improved housing, recreation facilities, health care, and control of crime and drug distribution have seldom been kept, even by the most sincere and honest community leaders. Disadvantaged people want to share in the planning of consistent and comprehensive efforts to alleviate concerns, to participate in the actual improvement of their own neighborhood, or to exert authority or influence over decisions that affect them.

The Atlanta Project will attempt to provide a bright

vision of the future that will inspire broad participation, will help to develop maximum involvement, assessment, and control of betterment programs by people in the troubled areas, and will support and encourage the expansion of ongoing efforts that have already proven to be successful.

V. When layoffs occur or when scarce jobs become available, the chronically unemployed fare worst. These often potentially good workers are not able to compete successfully with others who may be better educated, have been raised in families where the work ethic prevails, are familiar with labor rules and skilled in the preparation of job applications, have personal transportation to work sites, or regular access to notices of employment opportunities. Many employers do not make a special effort to compensate for these handicaps in their hiring practices.

The Atlanta Project will strive to promote a closer relationship between employers and would-be workers in the low-income neighborhoods, beginning at least as early as the high school years. We will also help train potential employees and encourage special efforts by business leaders to provide job opportunities in our targeted communities.

VI. Quite often, full-time professionals and volunteers are inadequately prepared to form effective partnerships and to carry out assignments that require understanding of cultural differences and the special circumstances of poverty or deprivation. Those who are most qualified by training and experience have limited opportunity to share their knowledge and advice with others. It is very difficult to generate an adequate sense of teamwork based on a clear understanding of common principles and goals.

The Atlanta Project will develop an extensive educational system, for general indoctrination and training of full-time workers and volunteers in specific tasks.

VII. Many grand designs for addressing inner-city problems fail because of inadequate sustained funding. The Atlanta Project will be financed mostly by existing resources, supplemented by a large number of volunteers and organizations. Contributions from foundations and businesses will be the source of our cash budget, more than half of which will be used to pay and support coordinators who will reside in and represent the targeted cluster communities. Our requests to government leaders will not emphasize funding, but we will seek flexibility and coordination among existing programs to ensure greater efficiency in developing better lives for poorer families.

The difficulty of creating and maintaining improvements in the inner cities has been demonstrated repeatedly. Basic changes are needed, including a raising of educational levels for children and adults, improved job opportunities, repair and beautification of neighborhoods, and the generation of confidence and self-reliance through incremental successes. These can lead to a reduction in prejudice or discrimination against the poor, and result in a cooperative spirit that can change our entire community. In many ways we are exploring uncharted territory, with no guarantee of success, but we will not permit the uncertainties and known difficulties to deter us.

INDEX

✯✯✯✯✯✯✯✯✯✯✯✯✯✯✯✯✯✯✯✯✯✯✯✯✯✯✯✯✯✯✯✯✯✯✯

ABOUT THE TYPE

The text of this book was set in Janson, a typeface designed by Anton Janson who was a punch cutter in seventeenth-century Germany. Janson is an excellent old-style book face with pleasing clarity and sharpness in its design.